CM0082591I

THE SCOTTISH POOR LAW
1745-1845

To S.G.C. and E.O.A.C.
whose encouragement helped
to make this book a reality

THE SCOTTISH
POOR LAW
1745-1845

R. A. CAGE

Department of Economic History
University of New England, N.S.W.

1981

SCOTTISH ACADEMIC PRESS
EDINBURGH

Published by
Scottish Academic Press Ltd
33 Montgomery Street, Edinburgh EH7 5JX

First published 1981
SBN 7073 0289 7

Printed in Great Britain by
REDWOOD BURN LIMITED
Trowbridge & Esher

CONTENTS

LIST OF TABLES AND MAPS

INTRODUCTION

The aim of this book is to analyse the effectiveness of the Scottish poor law in the century between 1745 and 1845 and to understand the social forces which brought about its change in 1845. Rather than concentrate on a detailed study of a particular area, the approach is a general one, treating Scotland as a whole. This is made practicable by the selection of a random sample of parishes through the whole of Scotland, and on this basis making a careful examination of their experience.

The century (1745-1845) was one of radical change for Scotland. It witnessed the fastest rates of increase in population in Scotland's history, rising from 1,265,380 in 1755 to 2,620,184 in 1841. It was a period of rapid industrialisation, with the resulting growth of urban areas and improvements in communication. Severe employment problems were caused by depressions in 1819, 1825-6, 1829, 1832, 1837 and 1840-3. In the light of these events it is surprising that the Scots' traditional views of the causes of poverty did not change. So far as the Lowlands were concerned, few contemporary Scottish observers seem to have made a serious attempt to relate the problem of poverty to the great changes being engendered by the industrial revolution. Concerning the specific causes of indigence in Scotland few writers defined them in terms of economics. Poverty was largely taken to be the result of personal behaviour and "moral degradation".

But in spite of the inadequacy of the provision it seems reasonable to conclude that the structure and intents of the pre-1845 Scottish system of poor relief contained much that was humane. Many facets of the practices which evolved, such as parochial visitation and education for the poor, were admirable. But the system between 1745 and 1845 became increasingly harsh, as it failed to cope with the rapidly changing structure of society resulting from industrialisation and

urbanisation, a process disruptive of the older social bonds and
productive of precariousness through trade fluctuations. The self-
help philosophy of the administrators was moralistic rather than
environmental. By blaming destitution on personal behaviour and
morality, rather than on the conditions within which they had to
operate, theorists, politicians, and administrators failed to make the
crucial link between destitution and unemployment, a factor often
beyond personal control. Furthermore, by inducing the view among the
labourers themselves that the taking of public assistance was a badge
of disgrace, the number of applications was severely limited. The
funds available for distribution were restricted by equating the
imposition of a legal assessment with the degeneration of the moral
standards of the poor. As the administrators of poor relief were also
the moral guardians of the community, it was convenient for them to
equate low poor relief doles with a high moral standard and to express
their satisfaction when no one applied for aid. Yet in this environment social change occurred and by the late 1820s a group of concerned
individuals emerged, who challenged the basic philosophy of the
Scottish system of poor relief. They observed and recorded a
connection between destitution, unemployment, poor living conditions,
and ill-health. Their arguments won the day, causing changes in the
legislation in 1845. The economic and social conditions of mid-
nineteenth century Scotland were radically different than those of the
mid-eighteenth century.

The logical starting point for a poor law study is to determine
the relevant system of legal rules and provisions. Chapter One
establishes the legal framework upon which the Scottish poor law rested.
As all poor law legislation in Scotland was completed prior to 1745, it
is necessary to exceed the specified time limits in order to gain an
understanding of the problems to be encountered.

Chapters Two and Three present and evaluate the available evidence concerning poor law practice. Chapter Two concentrates on the rural experience, relying primarily on the kirk session minutes and heritors' records. The urban scene is dealt with in Chapter Three, the records examined being town council proceedings and workhouse minutes. The Scottish poor law consisted of two sub-systems, the rural and the urban. Even though this dichotomy was initially the result of the legislation, the pressures of urbanisation and industrialisation caused the division to be more marked. Prior to 1750 the burghs studied were so small that poor relief administration in them could not be distinguished from that in the rural parishes, as the magistrates and town councils of the burghs usually delegated their administrative responsibilities to the Church. But as the population of the burghs increased and became more dense, the Church as administrator was either replaced or supplemented by elected lay officials. The rural system of relief in Scotland was less harsh than that in the urban areas; it was more responsive to the pauper's needs. Both rural and urban modes failed to provide an adequate subsistence, but much can be said in favour of a paternalistic approach of the rural kind, where the poor's requirements are better known.

Any study of a poor law system in isolation from other forms of charity and other systems would be sterile. Therefore, Chapter Four looks at the role of private charity, stressing its importance as the major means of relieving the poor. Chapter Five compares Scottish methods with those of England, though implicit comparisons are made throughout the whole of the work. The differences which evolved are significant and will prove useful to the students of the English poor law.

The first five Chapters thus present and analyse the workings of the Scottish poor law, 1745-1845. They represent the most comprehensive study available for the time period. After 1815 the existing tenets became an emotive rather than a rational topic of discussion. The course of the debate and eventual amendment of the law is traced through the final three Chapters.

Chapter Six studies the work of Thomas Chalmers and his Glasgow experiment, which largely ignored the social effects of industrialisation and urbanisation. Chalmers was a dedicated follower of the Scottish parochial form of relief, but he failed to grasp that it was not appropriate to the new urban context.

Chapter Seven is crucial for an understanding of the forces which prolonged a dying system and those which caused its amendment. Major reliance has been placed upon the General Assembly Reports of 1818 and 1839, the parliamentary debates, the work of W. P. Alison and Patrick Brewster. By 1840 it was inevitable that changes would be made; the process was quickened by the Disruption of the Church of Scotland in 1843.

The final Chapter deals with the massive Report of 1844 and the Amendment Act of 1845. Despite the Report's criticisms, few major revisions were recommended. In fact the 1845 Act did little to improve the lot of the poor in Scotland.

Perhaps the major shortcoming of the present approach is the difficulty of measuring the effectiveness of the operation of the law. This is due primarily to a lack of information concerning income and employment levels in Scotland for the period under consideration, and to the nature of the limited poor law data, making it impossible to determine the degree or seriousness of destitution. Without this knowledge it is gratuitous to condemn the apparent niggardly low allowances granted. Nevertheless it is possible to form an understanding of how the Scottish poor law system operated and to gain an appreciation of how the intensification of the market economy influenced both the level of average expenditure and the number of paupers. A study of this nature will also pinpoint the shortcomings in related fields, enabling researchers to determine where their efforts should be concentrated.

In writing this book I have incurred many debts, not all of which can be acknowledged here. However, particular appreciation must be expressed to Professor S. G. Checkland, Mrs E. O. A. Checkland, and Professor Anthony Slaven. Their lively criticisms helped to fashion and improve the text as it gradually took shape. The staffs of many libraries and depositories were unfailingly generous with their time and assistance, a special debt being incurred to Miss Jack, formerly of the University of Glasgow Library, Mrs Manchester, Baillie's Library, Glasgow, Dr W. Makey, City Archivist, Edinburgh, and to all the staff of Register House, Edinburgh. Of course this work would not have progressed without the careful typing done by Rosemary Heffernan and Sue Hombsch, and especially to Leanne Wunsch, who prepared the final typescript. Finally, thanks must be given to the thousands of Scots, who warmly welcomed an 'alien' and made me feel at home during my three year stay and my several return trips.

R. A. Cage
University of New England
Australia

The Scots had their own system of poor relief with its unique features, a system based upon various statutes of the Scottish Parliament as interpreted by the Court of Session. Between 1707 and 1845, Westminster did not add to this legislation. From an examination of the Scottish 'Acts anent the Poor' the intentions embodied in them will emerge. When these have been considered, it will be possible to determine whether or not the design they suggest was implemented between 1745 and 1845.

It is no mere antiquarian exercise to consider the course of Scottish poor law legislation. Rather, it is essential for an understanding of the poor in the century after 1745. For the problem and its treatment were in continuous evolution, producing a pattern full of variety and anomaly. In principle the law was the final arbiter, but in practice there was much confusion and complexity. Important insights into social phenomena can be gained by examining the course of legislation. Frequently additional acts must be passed because of the ineffectualness of preceding laws, the very lack of comprehensiveness of which is a reflection of the complexity of the social circumstances. But unfortunately attempts to simplify the procedure often introduce an element of ambiguity into the legislation by causing inconsistency between the statutes; further difficulty can arise if the meaning of the legislation is changed by the interpretation of the courts. Thus it is not surprising if the intent of the statutes is not always implemented. This can be the case especially if there is no central administration of the legislation.

Scottish laws against vagabonds were passed as early as 1424, when, during the reign of James I, there were several enactments intended to repress them. An Act in 1424 created an important distinction between those who were able to earn their own livelihood, and those who were obliged to resort to the charity of others for their subsistence. It directed that no person between the ages of fourteen and seventy years be allowed to beg, unless they could not earn their living by any other means; all those permitted to beg were to be issued with badges; while all others were to find employment or be burnt on the check and banished. Begging thus became an activity requiring official authority and controlled by strong sanctions. This Act was followed by another in 1425, which ordered the sheriffs to arrest all idle men, and after releasing them to allow them forty days to find employment; if such persons failed to procure employment within the forty day period, they were to be imprisoned and punished at the king's will. It would appear that these Acts were not always put into execution, as an Act passed in 1427 directed that an enquiry be made and a fine levied on all magistrates who failed to enforce them. Other Acts against vagabonds were passed in 1449, 1455, 1457, and 1477.

Even though these Acts are important, none except that of 1424 contains any mention of the 'legal poor'. An Act in 1503, further defining those individuals who were to enjoy the privilege of begging, stated that only those who were crippled, blind, impotent, or weak were to be allowed to beg. This was followed in 1535 by further restrictions upon the privileged class of licensed beggars by the enactment that no person would be allowed to beg in any parish other than that of his birth. Thus, it was established that each parish was to maintain its own poor.

The basis of the Scottish poor law is the Act of 1574, entitled 'Anent the Punishment of Strong and Idle Beggars and Provision for Sustentation of the Poor and Impotent'. The preamble of the Act declared that various Acts had been passed providing for the punishment of strong and idle beggars and a provision for the poor, such that none between the ages of fourteen and seventy years be allowed to beg. The Act continued by stating that the legal poor shall be allowed to beg only in the parish of their birth, where the parish officials were to make badges and give them to the individuals of their parish who were eligible to beg. It was ordered that if any person gave money, lodgings, or other forms of relief to a badgeless beggar, after being convicted of the said act, he should be fined an amount not exceeding five pound Scots (8s. 4d. Sterling) to be used for the lawful poor of the parish. The parish officials were to appoint one or more men to search out and imprison every vagabond in the parish.

Having dealt with strong and idle beggars, the next matter of concern was to allow provision for the legal poor, that is, all crippled, sick, impotent, and weak folk and those under fourteen years of age and over seventy who were unable to maintain themselves except by begging. To facilitate this, the justices in every parish were to prepare a list of their poor and then to ascertain their individual needs. After this had been done the parish residents were to be taxed according to their substance, the resulting funds to be used to provide for the poor. This was the first mention in the statutes of a source of funds for the poor; thus, it must be noted that the principle of an assessment was established before a reliance was placed upon voluntary contributions. If it was found to be inconvenient to collect money, the assessment could be paid in victuals, meat, and drink.

In order that a person might be able to return to his parish of birth or residence, provision was made for transportation. The officials of the pauper's current parish of residence were to provide him with a certificate indicating his parish of birth or legal residence. This certificate was to allow the pauper to pass from parish to parish, receiving aid from each, until he arrived at his destination, each parish traversed sharing in the pauper's travelling expenses. These expenses were paid as a further means of preventing unlicensed begging. It must be emphasised that the Act did not contain a provision for forcible removal. A person only had to report to his parish of birth or legal residence if he desired to be placed upon the rolls, and at no time could a person be forced to leave a parish if he applied for relief. Any pauper who was able to work, so as to earn part of his livelihood, was ordered to find suitable employment. If he refused to seek employment, he was to be placed in the stocks until he changed his mind. The same punishment was to be suffered by any beggar refusing to return to his parish of birth or legal residence.

The authors of the Act clearly felt that one method of eliminating the problems caused by begging was to remove the children of beggars from the influence of their parents. It was commonly believed at the time that once a child was taught the art of begging, he would always resort to that means of gaining a livelihood (indicating, perhaps, that begging was a profitable occupation). Hence, it was ordained that if a beggar had children between the ages of five and fourteen, any person of honest estate could take them into his service. The period of indenture was to last until the age of eighteen for females and twenty-four for males.

The Act of 1574, therefore, established a system of poor relief, clearly defining the proper recipients of public relief and the means of providing the relief, establishing the principle of an assessment as a source of funds and ordaining the period of legal residence as seven years. The administration of these laws devolved upon the provosts and bailies, justices and sheriffs.

Rather than continue with a chronology of the laws it will be more fruitful to analyse the system in the context of the following components: the administration of relief, the sources of funds for relief, the proper recipients of relief, the setting of the poor to work, and the parish of settlement and liability. Each component will

be reviewed according to its treatment by the law, as provided by the
statutes and decisions of the Court of Session, prior to the passage
of the Poor Law Amendment Act (Scotland) in 1845.

A. *The Administration of Relief*

In 1574 the administration of poor relief was placed in the hands
of the provost and bailies of the burghs and the justices in landward
parishes; the sheriffs had an overall responsibility to ensure that the
Act was duly executed in their shires, both the rural and urban parts.
The power of administering relief in rural parishes was transferred to
the particular session of the kirk by the Act of 1597 and reinforced by
the Act of 1672, which also made the heritors, who had been entrusted
with the power of levying assessments for employing vagabonds and idle
beggars, jointly responsible with the sessions in the administration of
the law.

The kirk session for each parish was the lowest ecclesiastical
court in the Church of Scotland. It was composed of the parish
minister and elders. Besides their legal responsibilities towards the
poor, the session also supervised the religious and moral character of
the parishioners. The heritors were all persons possessing heritable
property within the parish, usually excluding houses. Heritors could
also serve as elders, creating a situation whereby the heritors'
interests were represented even though they did not actively partake
in the management of the poor's fund.

Finally, the Proclamations of the Privy Council on 11th August
1692, 29th August 1693, and 3rd March 1698, which were ratified by
Parliament in 1698, confirmed the powers granted to the heritors and
kirk sessions in landward parishes and to the magistrates in the
burghs. These officials were also granted the authority to decide and
determine all questions not determined by the Acts of Parliament or by
Proclamations of the Privy Council, which might arise in their

respective parishes in relation to the ordering and disposing of the poor.

According to Scottish law the Court of Session rules on the legality of all legislation pertaining to Scotland if the provisions of an Act are ever questioned. With respect to poor relief the Court of Session was the only authority to which contesting parties could appeal. Therefore rulings by the Court would either uphold previous interpretations of the law, clarify them, or change them. Hence, it is necessary to review Court cases in order to determine the status of the legislation concerning poor relief. The first decision of the Court of Session respecting the administration of the law was on 15th February, 1751 in the case of the heritors of the parish of Humbie, Haddingtonshire, against the minister and kirk session. The Lords found

> That the heritors have a joint right and power with the kirk session in the administration, management, and distribution, of all and every of the funds belonging to the poor of the parish, as well collections as sums mortified for the use of the poor, and stocked out upon interest, and have right to be present and join with the session in their administration, distributing, and employment of such sums; without prejudice to the kirk-session to proceed in their ordinary and incidental charities, though the heritors be not present nor attend.[1]

It was further declared that any extraordinary administration or uplifting of funds should be announced from the pulpit ten days in advance, so that the heritors might have an opportunity to attend. This ruling was amplified in 1752, when the Court ordained that any of the heritors of a parish were entitled to call the kirk session to account for their management of the poor's fund.[2] Another ruling which confirmed the heritors' and kirk sessions' right to administration was made in 1772, with a decision that the sheriff had no power to judge of the amount of aliment to be awarded to a pauper.[3] The only time that the sheriff had jurisdiction was when the sessions failed to meet to decide on a claim; in that situation, the sheriff could order the session to meet,[4] but, once the session had done so, the sheriff had no power to alter or review the orders or judgment of the session.[5] In 1824 it was declared that the heritors and kirk session in their administration of the poor law were subject to the control of the Court of Session.[6]

It is clear then that the kirk session and heritors were jointly responsible for the administration of poor relief in rural parishes, though neither party could meet for that purpose without notifying the other. If, after being duly informed of a meeting to impose an assessment, the heritors failed to appear, the kirk session was free to take action; the sessions, however, were accountable to the heritors, who could appoint representatives to attend the meeting on their behalf. The sheriff of the shire had no powers in the matter except to enforce upon the administrators, if necessary, the discharge of their duty. Finally, the administrators were subject to the rulings of the Court of Session, to which any aggrieved party could appeal.

B. *The Sources of Funds for Relief*

There were two main sources of funds for relief, voluntary collections and legal assessments. As has already been stated, the Act of 1574 ordered the parish officials to determine the necessary weekly amount to sustain their poor and then tax and stent the inhabitants, according to their means and substance, in order to raise the necessary funds; the taxation and stent rolls were to be reviewed annually. The Act of 1625 required each parish to place a stent upon the rent paid in the parish and upon each farmer and householder according to his means and substance, the heritors having to pay the stent levied by the parish regardless of where they lived. This was followed by an Act in 1663, which declared that one half of the assessment was to be paid by the heritors and the other half by the tenants and inhabitants.

Voluntary contributions as a source of funds were not specifically mentioned in the statutes until the Privy Council Proclamation of 29th August, 1693. It ordained that half of the sums collected at parish churches and dues received by the session were to be made available for the poor. It should be noted that, although the use of the other half of the collections was not specified, the money was generally made available for temporary assistance to the poor. Even though no mention was made of voluntary contributions until 1693, it was implicit that they should compose a portion of the funds. This is the case since the Act of 1574 stated that the assessment was to be imposed to meet deficiencies in the funds. As no other major source of funds was mentioned, it must be assumed that voluntary contributions would be acceptable and, indeed, expected. Mortifications to the poor were another source of voluntary contributions, as were marriage proclamation fees and mortcloth dues.

Fines appear in the statutes as a third source of funds. The Act of 1574 provided that fines imposed by special statutes for offences against the peace were to belong to the poor, as were fines imposed on individuals giving alms to beggars from other parishes, and the Privy Council Proclamation of 11th August, 1692, ordained that the penalties on parishes neglecting to enforce the laws on poor relief and fines imposed on individuals refusing to give their fair quota were also to belong to the poor. There is no indication that such fines were ever imposed.

The right of the heritors and sessions in landward parishes and of bailies and magistrates in burghs to levy an assessment was never questioned in the Court of Session, but there were cases concerning the mode of assessment and the extent of liability. Surprisingly, the Court ruled in 1773 that, for the maintenance of the poor, the heritors had the power to assess in accordance with the real rent, where that was expedient, although the practice may have been to levy according to the traditional or 'valued' rent. With respect to the extent of liability, the Court ruled that a person could be assessed on their heritable property within the parish and on their personal estate wherever situated.

With respect to church collections, there were only two court cases. The first, that of 1739, concerned the collections of dissenting meeting houses. In this case the Court ruled that their collections were not to be appropriated for the support of the poor, but were to be at the sole disposal of the congregation. This case was a result of the Established Church's diminished collections owing to the first secession from the Church. The Established Church was responsible for providing legal assistance. In the second case, in 1839, the Court decided that churches of the Establishment, built by voluntary contributions, still had to pay one-half of their collections to the poor's fund.

C. *The Proper Recipients of Relief*

As already mentioned, an Act in 1503 declared that only crippled, blind, impotent, and weak folk were to enjoy the privilege of begging. This can be considered the first enactment making provision for the legal poor, that is those entitled to beg, albeit they were, when possible, to fend for themselves. The Act of 1535 restricted this privileged class to begging only in their parish of birth. The first act to provide for public maintenance of the poor was that of 1574. Every parish was to provide lodging and abiding places for all their aged, impotent, and poor people, a definition of persons eligible for relief which remained unchanged for nearly a century. A new definition, or rather, a clarification, was contained in the Act of 1661: no person was to receive public relief, who was able in any way to earn his own livelihood. Lists were to be made of all poor, aged, sick, lame, and impotent inhabitants of the parish, who were unable to work or in any way maintain themselves. Relief was also to be given to all orphans and other poor children left destitute of all help within the parish. Thus, in the same Act the classes of individuals eligible for public relief were expanded, and the denial of the able-bodied unemployed to relief seemingly was re-affirmed.

Considerable confusion can arise with respect to the legal status of granting relief to the able-bodied. As the statutes given above (particularly that of 1661) clearly define those eligible for public assistance, and as the able-bodied are not included, it has been argued that they were not entitled to public relief by implication. It could also be argued that the Act of 1661 explicitly excluded the able-bodied, stating that no person was to receive public relief if he was able to earn his own livelihood. It should be noted, however, that the Act of 1661 did not exclude the possibility of the able-bodied receiving public assistance during times of temporary disability. Perhaps this was responsible for the practice which developed of classifying paupers as being either "regular" or "occasional". Hence, it was common to find on the parish pauper lists able-bodied individuals receiving temporary assistance because of illness or other temporary disabilities, other than unemployment. This practice was viewed as a legitimate function of the administrators, as it helped to prevent people in temporary need becoming a permanent burden on the funds. It is not clear from the records the source of funds for relieving such occasional paupers. It must be remembered, however, that each session had at its disposal the one-half of the church collections not legally belonging to the poor. Therefore, the payments to the occasional pauper may have come from these funds. Whether this was the case cannot be determined because parishes did not separate their collections. But even this distinction is not necessary to make, for a labourer with, say, a broken leg would be unable to maintain himself, thus being eligible by reason of temporary disability for relief. It is clear, however, that the able-bodied because of unemployment were not relieved from the funds, but rather from special collections or voluntary subscriptions called for this purpose. Therefore, the standard practice during the period under consideration of granting relief to the able-bodied during times of temporary distress, other than unemployment, may not have been inconsistent with the law.

The only Court of Session case questioning the right of the able-bodied to receive relief from the public funds occurred in 1804, in the Case of Pollock against Darling.[7] The Court found by a majority of one that

> Those persons are entitled to relief under the system of poor-laws, who, tho' in ordinary seasons able to gain their livelihood, are reduced during a dearth of provisions to have recourse to a charitable supply; and an extraordinary assessment may for that purpose be levied.

In the case Darling argued that the poor derive their right to public support from the law: he was not against the imposition of a legal assessment to maintain those entitled to relief. However, he was opposed to the granting of assistance to the able-bodied. The problem arose because crop failures in 1799 and 1800 caused the price of meal to rise substantially. It was therefore thought necessary to provide temporary assistance to many not upon the poor's roll. Accordingly, an extraordinary assessment was imposed upon the parish inhabitants. The parish of Dunse had had an assessment for nearly a century. For the period in question the parish kept two distinct lists, the "Regular Poor" and the "Industrious Poor". The assessments for the two classes were also kept distinct. The parish argued that the

> inability to earn subsistence, is the true and only distress which it is the object of a code of poor's laws to relieve. The causes which produce this disability, provided they be

> real, cannot be distinguished from each other. Vice may
> have brought on infirmity, and idleness may have created a
> disability to labour: Still such misfortunes would be
> relieved: And shall not assistance be afforded to the
> honest and industrious man who worked diligently, and yet
> is unable, from the circumstances of the times, to save
> himself and his family from want?

This decision opened the door to the able-bodied unemployed to claim
relief as a legal right. As might be expected, the Court's decision
was not unanimous, for many were worried that a dangerous precedent
was established.

The Pollock-Darling Case arose simply because the funds were
obtained from a legal assessment, even though this assessment was ear-
marked for a specific purpose. Darling was not questioning the
appropriateness of granting assistance to the able-bodied during
periods of temporary disability. Rather, he was against providing
relief to the able-bodied unemployed from a legal assessment instead
of a voluntary source of funds. This is an important distinction to
bear in mind when assessing whether the Case represented a change in
attitude towards granting relief to the able-bodied. The former
position had long been a tradition in Scotland and had developed
within the framework of the law. The latter position had always been
alien to Scottish practice, as the able-bodied unemployed had
traditionally been aided by voluntary public subscriptions held
outwith the framework of the Scottish poor law. In spite of the
favourable ruling, the parishes continued to deny the able-bodied
unemployed public relief, leading to intensive debates during periods
of massive industrial unemployment in urban areas, particularly
Paisley. Thus in effect the acuteness of the inadequacy of the
poor law was only felt after the development of industrial urban
areas.

Unfortunately, Pollock-Darling was the only case of this nature
heard by the Court before the passage of the Poor Law Amendment Act

(Scotland) in 1845, though in 1821, a petition to the heritors and session of Abbey Parish of Paisley by 825 able-bodied men claiming relief as poor, because of a need arising from a stagnation of manufacturing employment, was refused by the heritors on the grounds that these individuals were not legally entitled to relief. The men appealed to the sheriff, who ordered the heritors and session to assess themselves in order to provide relief to the men. The heritors and session appealed to the Court of Session, which reversed the sheriff's decision on the grounds that his action was beyond his jurisdiction; the unemployed men should have petitioned the Court. For some unknown reason the men did not file a petition with the Court; perhaps more jobs were by then available, thus eliminating any need to pursue the matter.

The position with respect to the eligibility of the able-bodied poor for relief in Scotland may be summarised as follows, taking as a starting point the sources of funds. There were four possible directions from which money for the relief of paupers might come.

The first was the parish assessment, in effect a tax on the landed property in the parish. This was the sole point in poor law matters at which the sanction of law attached. The phrase in the Act of 1661 governing the matter excluded any persons who were in any way able to gain their own living. This phrase may be interpreted in physical terms, as referring to age or disability, or in employment terms, as referring to the possibility of finding a job. The physical interpretation conformed more closely to the tenor of the times, and so the phrase might be taken to exclude the able-bodied. But an ambiguity could still be argued to be present, allowing of the relief of those who were able-bodied but out of employment. It is certainly clear, however, that there was no positive entitlement on the part of the able-bodied to relief on employment grounds, as could

14.

be claimed in the English case.

The next possible source of relief funds was from the collections taken at church doors. Such collections were, of course, a matter of voluntary giving, with no legal sanctions applied. They were in fact the normal source of Scottish poor relief. The collections were divided conceptually into two parts, though in the examples found this was not done in the bookkeeping sense. To the first half of the collection the poor were entitled; indeed it was specifically for their benefit. The claim of the able-bodied to a share was governed by the same principles as affected the assessment.

The second half of such collections was at the discretion of the kirk sessions; such monies had to serve the general needs of the parish, including the maintenance of the church fabric. From this part of the collections, using their discretionary power, the kirk sessions could relieve able-bodied persons, certainly over temporary disability and also, as in some observed cases, over periods of unemployment or other economic difficulty. In so doing the kirk session would, as appears from examples recorded in the minutes, designate such persons 'occasional poor'.

The fourth and final possible source of aid for the able-bodied was voluntary funds raised by interested persons. These, being entirely outside the poor law provision and the kirk, could be used for the able-bodied at the discretion of those administering such funds. Indeed their principle origin lay in times of large scale unemployment.

In sum, then, the Scottish poor law certainly made no explicit provision for the able-bodied, but indeed, could reasonably be taken to have denied it, though not in unambiguous terms. Both of the sources of relief on which the able-bodied unemployed could hope to draw (the discretionary half of the collection and funds raised by appeals and subscriptions outside the church) were additional to the poor law provision as enforceable at law. In such a complex situation it is hardly surprising that anomalies occurred, and that the relation between law and practice was not a simple one.

D. *The Setting of the Poor to Work*

The statutes contain provision for setting both the legal poor and the idle beggars to work. As previously mentioned, the Act of 1574 ordained that any poor able to work to earn part of their subsistence, should be ordered to work. Furthermore, any person of honest estate was entitled to take into his service any beggars' children between the ages of five and fourteen. The Act of 1597 added the clause that strong beggars and their children were to be employed in common works. According to the Act of 1625, each parish was to provide a house where their poor could be gainfully employed.

With respect to setting idle beggars to work, the Acts are even more numerous, and are concerned with both the idle beggars and their children. The first was passed in 1617 and dealt with the children of beggars acquiring the custom of begging and hence becoming beggars. Thus it was considered good and profitable if individuals or corporations would take these children away from their parents, employ them in some occupation, and provide them with an education. The conditions were that the children must be certified by the provost and bailies in the burghs and by the kirk session in landward parishes to the effect that they were poor and unable to maintain themselves. If the child was under fourteen, he was required to receive the advice of the magistrates or session. His period of service was to last until the age of thirty. Again, in 1641, in order to encourage the development of new manufactures and to rid the country of beggars, a commission was established to encourage manufacturers and to establish wages for apprehended beggars. Besides being able to apprehend them for employment, the manufacturers were also to receive concessions in that they need pay neither import duties on raw materials nor tax. The Act of 1649 ordered that all able-bodied beggars were to be apprehended and put to work. There is no evidence that correction houses were established or that manufacturers seized beggars for the purpose of putting them to work. Hence, it is not surprising that there was no court cases dealing with the setting of the poor to work.

E. *The Parish of Settlement and Liability*

The statutes provide only for birth and residence as qualifications for obtaining a settlement, the period of residence necessary to acquire a settlement vacillating between seven and three years. A means of assisting a pauper voluntarily en route to his parish of settlement was established by the Act of 1574. This statute provided that the pauper was to be given a certificate by his parish of residence in order that he could obtain aid from those parishes he traversed on his way to his parish of settlement. Although the laws are quite clear as to settlement, the practice in this area was determined by court decisions. Thus, in order to determine whether settlements acquired from birth and residence could be delegated to wives and children of the parties acquiring them the courts came to recognize marriage and parentage as two further sources of settlement. Furthermore, the burden of maintaining a pauper could not be thrown on the parish of his birth if he had acquired a settlement in another way. The decision of the Court was that the parish in which an indigent person had resided for a period of three years, immediately preceding his application for relief, was bound to provide relief to him. Hence, the period requisite for a settlement was established at three years.

Another important matter which became law through court decisions concerned the liability of a parish for providing relief, that is the circumstances in which an individual was eligible for parish assistance. Generally, the Court held that the parish became liable only if the applicants' relatives were unable to support them: children were bound to support their parents and paternal and maternal ascendants; likewise, the parents were bound to support their children, as were the grandparents; but a son's parents were not required to maintain his wife after his death.

F. *Summary*

From the preceding comments it should be clear that Scotland, from the fifteenth century, had a system of poor relief established by statute and elaborated by Court rulings, and by 1745, well defined. The laws were administered by the magistrates and town council in burghs and by the heritors and kirk session in rural areas, these local officials being regarded as closer to the problems of people and knowing their needs; but if these failed to fulfil their duties, the Court of Session could order them to supply relief. Persons eligible for relief were orphans and deserted children under the age of fourteen, individuals over seventy, and the severely disabled, all of whom could receive relief only as a last resort. In order that a parish be liable for relief of an individual he had to acquire a settlement obtained by a continuous residence of three years in a parish, or, failing that, such settlement was determined by the paupers' place of birth. Funds for relief were obtained from voluntary contributions and from legal assessments. One-half of the church collections were to be applied to the support of the poor. If all contributions taken together were not sufficient, the parish had the duty of imposing a legal assessment, levied twice yearly by the heritors and kirk session. One-half of the assessed amount was to be paid by the heritors and the other half by the inhabitants of the parish.

18.

These were the various elements of the system as contained in the laws. The prevailing philosophy of the period produced, as another component of the system, a belief that the amount received by paupers should be less than the earnings of the lowest paid workers, thus, the principle of 'less eligibility', made so famous by the English Act of 1834, was fundamental to the traditional Scottish principles. This, combined with the reliance placed upon relatives and neighbours, served to place a stigma upon the reception of public relief. The receipt of such relief involved a moral judgment by society. These feelings were probably strengthened by the Church's attitude during the eighteenth and early nineteenth centuries that the cause of pauperism was due to a lack of moral fibre. Pauperism could not be eliminated by providing individuals with a subsistence level of living, but only by instilling into them the virtues of a moral, Christian life.

---

1. William Morison, *The Decisions of the Court of Session*, vol. 25-26, p. 10,556.

2. Morison, p. 10,570.

3. Morison, p. 10,577.

4. *Cases*, Kirk Session of Glassford *v*. Orr, 10th July, 1827, 5 S., p. 921.

5. *Cases*, Clader *v*. Trotter, 8th June, 1833, 11 S., p. 694.

6. *Cases*, Higgins *v*. Kirk Session of the Barony, 9th July, 1824, 3 S., p. 239.

7. William Morison, pp. 10591-2.

In rural areas the law of Scotland placed the responsibility for administering relief to the poor jointly with the heritors and kirk sessions of each parish. These two groups were held liable for levying funds and supplying the needs of those requiring public assistance. If such funds could not be obtained by voluntary collections, an assessment was to be imposed. Only the orphaned young, the aged, and the impotent were to receive relief; the able-bodied unemployed apparently were never recognized by the statutes as being proper recipients of public support. This was the legal frame-work, but what was the practice? As there were nearly 850 rural parishes in Scotland, the possibility existed of great variety in the law's implementation. Who was given relief? How and when were they paid? How much did they receive? What were the sources of the funds? What were the attitudes of the administrators? Who were the adminis-trators? Answers to these and other questions will throw light upon the system of poor relief in Scotland for 1745-1845.

Ideally, every parish should be examined. But, since this would be impractical, a set of criteria must be established to permit a statistically valid examination. A random sample of two parishes from each county was taken and is listed in Table 1 and shown on Map 1. For some counties, particularly those in western Scotland, the selection of parishes was determined solely by the existence of adequate records. The result of this method was that few Highland parishes were examined in great detail. To overcome this defect, the two Statistical Accounts and the evidence in the 1818, 1839, and 1844 Reports were examined for a number of Highland parishes. The type of information which these sources provided was of a limited nature. Nonetheless, it was possible to determine that the general practice in

TABLE I: SCOTLAND: SAMPLE PARISHES AND BURGHS

(I)   *North and Western Scotland*

Ross and Cromarty: (1) Cromarty; (2) Kiltearn
Inverness: (3) Croy; (4) Cawdor; (5) Moy
Bute: (6) Kilmory; (7) Rothesay
Argyle: (8) Craignish; (9) Kilmore; (10) Dunoon
Caithness: (11) Canisbay; (12) Halkirk; (13) Reay
Sutherland: None
Orkney: (14) Sandwick

(II)   *Northeast Lowlands and Central Highlands*

Nairn: (4) Cawdor
Elgin: (15) Drainie; (16) Elgin
Banff: (17) Deskford; (18) Grange
Aberdeen: (19) Kenmay; (20) Tough
Kincardine: (21) Fordoun; (22) Nigg
Forfar: (23) Craig
Perth: (24) Aberfoyle; (25) Liff

(III) *East Coast Lowlands*

Fife: (26) Kilmany; (27) Anstruther Easter
Kinross: (28) Arngask; (29) Orwell
Clackmannan: None
Haddington: (30) Salton; (31) Tranent; (32) Dalkeith
Linlithgow: (33) Uphall; (34) Cramond
Edinburgh: (35) Cranstoun; (36) Newbattle

(IV)   *Central and Southwest Lowlands*

Stirling: (37) Falkirk; (38) Dunipace
Dumbarton: (39) Cardross; (40) Arrochar
Renfrew: (41) Eastwood
Ayr: (42) Ballantrae; (43) Sorn
Lanark: (44) Shotts; (45) Bothwell

(V)   *Southern Uplands*

Selkirk: None
Berwick: (46) Ayton; (47) Lauder
Peebles: (48) Manor; (49) Stobo
Roxburgh: (50) Sprouston; (51) Hounan
Dumfries: (52) Tynron; (53) Dumfries
Kirkcudbright: (54) Anwoth; (55) Kells
Wigton: (56) Mochrum; (57) Sorbie

Burghs

(a) Aberdeen
(b) Dundee
(c) Dumfries
(d) Glasgow
(e) Edinburgh (Royalty, Canongate, St. Cuthbert's)
(f) Paisley

Map1: Sample Parishes & Burghs

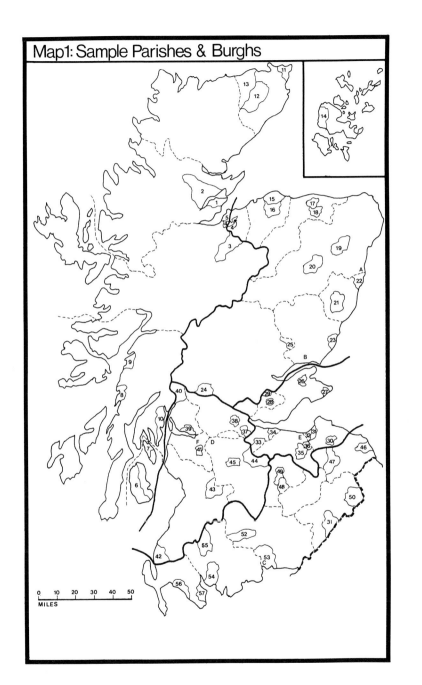

0 10 20 30 40 50
MILES

the Highlands was for the kirk sessions in each parish to make an annual distribution to those on the pauper lists from the scanty amount raised by church door collections. Some further light on Highland relief was gained from secondary source material and appears throughout the book.

The main sources used were the kirk session minutes and the heritors' records. Although they provided useful information, these documents also present problems. The kirk session minutes are primarily concerned with moral standards and often provide little information on poor relief matters. Even when the kirk session minutes contain entries concerning the poor, they are often unhelpful. The minutes rarely indicate the reason for the admission of a pauper to the list, only the name and amount of pension usually appear. Quite often individuals' names do not appear, only the date and total distribution being given. Thus, it is not possible to reconstruct the lists, especially since the death of a pauper rarely was recorded. As for other entries concerning the poor, the kirk session minutes seldom provide any rationale for a decision, only the fact that a decision was made and duly recorded. Fortunately, the heritors' records are more valuable for policy matters. But their usefulness is limited by the number available.

A. *Administration of Relief*

At the time of the 'forty-five' the law was not being enforced in the northern parishes despite the fact that orders were frequently given by the presbyteries and the sheriffs to the kirk sessions that the laws were to be put into operation. The heritors' role in the administration of relief in the northern regions is difficult to judge, as no heritors' minutes for these areas have been located. Some evidence does exist to suggest that the heritors were consulted during times of difficulties. They in their turn were only interested

when their pockets were affected. The only evidence that the
heritors took a more active part in the management of the poor was
for the parish of Craig, Forfarshire, where, because of the resignation of the elders in 1843 at the time of the Disruption, the kirk
session turned everything over to the heritors.

For the southern regions the heritors did take an active interest
in the management of the funds, their role being a two-fold one of
reviewing the actions of the session and having the final say in all
matters affecting the poor. The review often took the form of acting
as a rubber stamp, especially as most kirk sessions had a high
percentage of elders who were also heritors. Though the active
participation of the heritors increased with the imposition of a
legal assessment.

Attempts were often made to improve the administration and to
inform the elders and heritors of their legal responsibilities.
Sometimes this took the form of appealing to some authority, such as
the purchase of a copy of Dunlop's book on the poor law. Another
method was to inform the managers of their responsibilities. This is
shown by the following statement designed to decrease the poor's
rate:

> That the members shall be hereafter regularly and timeously
> cited to attend the meeting of session. That when assess-
> ments are ordered to be laid on, the exact sum specified
> shall be levied and no more. That in distributing money
> to the poor those only who are proper objects of charity
> shall receive relief and no sums of money shall in future
> be paid or sustained except upon proper orders duly
> authorized.[1]

This extract also illustrates another aspect of the Scottish system
of poor relief: the unwillingness in normal times to provide relief
to those other than the proper objects, as set forth in the law.

A final means of improving the efficiency of the management was
to divide the parish into districts, each assigned an elder familiar
with its inhabitants to investigate all applications for relief. As

sometimes happened, the elders were empowered in distant districts to look after their own poor, after consulting with the minister about their actions. The minister also was given power to order money from the treasurer for these cases. Furthermore, with the introduction of the assessment all functions of management were no longer gratis; paid clerks and collectors were hired. The officials collected the stent and paid the pensions according to the dictates of the managers.

In summary the kirk sessions and heritors did implement the poor law in rural areas. In every parish examined the kirk session took an active role, but in general the heritors were not involved until the threat of imposing a legal assessment. In many parishes the heritors from time to time led the fight to prevent a legal assessment; they were willing to impose a voluntary contribution among themselves to meet that end.

B. Sources of Funds

By law funds for the poor came from voluntary contributions in the form of one-half of the church door collections, fines, mortcloth dues, proclamation fees, mortifications and donations. When these voluntary sources were not sufficient, an assessment was to be laid, one-half payable by the heritors and the other half by the inhabitants.

All parishes examined used at least one-half of their church door collections to support their poor. Difficulties seemed to arise, particularly in remote areas where worn out or foreign coins were slipped into the collection. The situation was so bad in Croy that in 1771 a general distribution to the poor could not be made.[2] Crafty clergy resorted to the practice of 'handing around the ladle'; this exerted moral suasion as the contents of the ladle on its long handle were visible to all. It should be noted that most parishes paid their session clerk's salary out of the poor's fund. Furthermore, other incidental outlays were frequently made from the collections, indicating that the sessions made no distinction between the various types of expenditure. Nonetheless, it is impossible to indicate the extent to which the poor's fund suffered from such a practice, for only one-half of the church door collections belonged to the poor.

Fines and fees were also an important source of revenue, some parishes developing unusual ones in an attempt to prevent the imposition of a legal assessment, as, for example, a fee for the right to erect a headstone. This fee was quite common in the southern Lowland areas, where people appeared to have an obsession about making arrangements for permanently marking their own resting place before their death. The orthodox types of fines and fees were proclamation of marriage dues, fees for the use of the mortcloth, fines for irregular marriages and births, and fines for fornication. In certain cases fines imposed by the sheriff were given to the poor's funds, but usually only those fines imposed by the kirk session were included. Sessions went to great lengths to protect their right to impose fines and fees. It was reported in Sorn in 1830 that a society had been formed in the parish for the purpose of letting out mortcloths. As this action by the society would be detrimental to the poor's fund, the heritors decided that claims should be made in the small debt court in Ayr against any persons who have used, or may use, any such mortcloths.[3] Another puzzling item was the Church's apparent reliance on fines as a means of absolving sin. Perhaps it was felt that a person would suffer more in this life if his pocketbook was taxed, thus enabling him to enjoy greater benefits in his after life. But a better explanation is that the kirk session had the legal right to call any inhabitant of the parish before them, regardless of their affiliation. Therefore, the only effective punishment the session had for non-members was the imposition of a fine.

Sessions could impose a fine, but they could also forego its payment. In some parishes this procedure was common, as an entry of the following nature appeared quite frequently in the Fordoun, Kincardineshire session minutes: "Clementine Fraser, guilty of fornication. She paid down the usual penalty; but the Session upon account of her extreme indigence returned her the same by way of charity."[4] This is a rather curious entry in the light of the contemporary belief that loose morals were a primary cause of pauperism; such apparent encouragement of moral degradation perhaps increased the pauper rolls!

Donations and legacies (mortifications) also contributed to the make-up of the funds. Unless they were small in amount, the sums received were commonly invested, the yearly interest distributed to the poor. Smaller donations usually consisted of periodic gifts from the larger landlords, such as when the Earl of Ancrum gave a £10 donation to the poor of the parish, and particularly those in the villages of Newbattle, Easthouses, and Westhouses.[5] Of a more unusual nature was a donation from Duncan Davidson, who, upon being elected M.P., gave the session £30 for the poor,[6] or when Capt. James Inness of Canisbay gave £9 to the poor, so that they could celebrate his birthday in their own way.[7] Large donations were either invested in lands, lent out at interest for the benefit of the poor, or placed in some other interest-bearing business. Every attempt was made to keep these donations intact and to add to them; only the income from them was normally distributed to the poor, except during times of unusually severe distress. But it should be emphasised that the loans were not always made to good borrowers, for in Falkirk it was reported that £550 lent from the poor's fund to Mess. Rupel and Aitken had been lodged in the Commerical Bank in their names, and they refused to return it.[8]

Churches often constructed a loft, usually from money belonging to the poor. The seats were either made available to the poor, or, more likely, to other people with the amount of the seat rent placed in the poor's fund. In Croy the loft constructed for the poor was outfitted with pews, which were let out to the highest bidder, the receipts placed in the poor's fund.[9]

Whenever the church door collections and the revenue from the permanent fund were not sufficient to maintain the poor, either a voluntary subscription was made or a legal assessment imposed. A voluntary subscription could take two forms. The first was either a special collection within the church or a door to door collection within the parish. The other form that a voluntary collection could assume was an assessment which the heritors imposed on themselves in order to prevent the levying of a legal assessment. In most northern parishes at no time was it suggested when funds were low to impose a legal assessment; rather, solutions were adopted which hurt least in the short-run and avoided assessments. In the southern parishes there was also resistence to a legal assessment, but when it was realised that one was necessary, it was imposed. Even after a legal assessment was imposed, it was necessary to collect it. This sometimes proved to be very difficult, and recourse often was made to the courts in order to obtain the assessed amounts. The absentee heritors were a common problem. They did not contribute to the church collections and were loathe to fulfil any obligations towards the poor, giving rise to greater pressures to impose an assessment. This is clearly illustrated by the case of Grange, where the session realised that the funds at their disposal were barely sufficient to meet the needs of the poor. They resolved to bring these facts under the notice of those heritors and farmers connected with the parish, who, from non-residence or other causes, had not contributed to the parochial fund for the relief of the poor, and request that they make ". . . such voluntary annual contributions to the fund, as their several means will allow".[10]

Problems sometime arise in determining whether a parish was assessed, hence it is necessary to adhere to a strict set of definitions. A parish was not assessed if its funds for the poor were derived from voluntary contributions in the form of church collections or legacies. A parish was 'voluntarily' assessed if the heritors of the parish agreed to contribute among themselves a fixed amount for the support of the poor. A parish was 'legally' assessed if the kirk session and heritors laid a stent on the parish, usually with the heritors paying one-half and the inhabitants the other half. In the Scottish context only a parish with a 'legal' assessment can be classified as being an assessed parish. It was common practice for parishes to resort to a legal assessment only during times of difficulties; when the crisis was over, the assessment disappeared. Thus, when stating that a parish was assessed, it is necessary to include a date.

All the sources of funds as described in the laws were used, besides a few additional ones devised by several parishes. The greatest reliance was placed upon the voluntary sources; legal assessments were viewed as an evil, which were used only as a last resort and came into existence primarily after 1800, when severe pressures were continuously exerted upon the funds.

C. *Recipients of Relief and the Provision made for them*

From the administrator's point of view it was generally held that parochial relief should be regarded only as a last resort; people should look first to other means of maintaining themselves, particularly to their friends and relatives. However, if an individual could not obtain sufficient funds for his maintenance from other sources and if he was a proper object of charity, the parish would provide supplementary relief. It is interesting to note that evidence exists which indicates that the weekly allowance was frequently determined by the price of meal. Such a use of a sliding scale cost of living index was widely practiced in Scotland well before the adoption of the famous Speenhamland System in England.

Even if an individual was a proper object of relief, there was a stigma on being placed upon the fund, as the reception of public aid was considered to be morally degrading. This was an attitude the parishes often took advantage of in order to keep the numbers on the roll low. A favourite means, particularly in the Highlands, was to issue those on the roll with badges, which had to be visibly worn as long as the person received parochial assistance. In a number of parishes the badges were referred to as 'beggars badges', as the owner was given permission to beg within the parish bounds, usually only on certain days of the week, instead of receiving an allowance from the session. The badges were usually made of lead, pewter, copper, or cast iron, though stone badges were also known; in Grange in 1840, the badges were made out of pasteboard. It must be emphasised that the paupers were expected to wear the badges, and that the one for Cromarty was about six inches across and weighed eight ounces. The Cromarty session in 1757 paid two pence each for 60 badges, and ordered that, since the poor were unwilling to take them, none be given money from the poor's fund without a badge. Parishes also used the badges as a means of controlling begging by stranger poor, who apparently were a growing menace as the kirk session minutes frequently contained mention of begging poor from other parishes.

Not all parishes humiliated their poor, but few went as far to prevent it as the parish of Kemnay, Aberdeenshire, where, because the distribution of meal to the poor was causing "heartburn and uncandid reflections" by those entitled to it, the session felt that it "would be most conducive to the interest of religion and humanity to divide among the poor the money now in their hands, and let them procure meal for themselves wherever it can be got."[11] In another

northeast Lowland parish, Tough, the session judged it advisable to
lend small sums to some of the poor not on the roll and anxious not
to be identified with those on the fund.[12]

Individuals belonging to dissenting places of worship were often
denied relief from the parochial funds, even if they were eligible
for relief according to the law. The Grange session voted to inform
Mr. Young, minister of the Seceding Congregation that it was the
"... resolution of the Session 'that none of his poor for the
future are to be supplied from our funds unless he agree to reimburse
what is so given out'".[13] The Govan, Renfrewshire, heritors in a
question of giving relief to an orphan boy whose parents had been
members of the Relief Congregation, decided that the Relief
Congregation should care for him, and his claim was laid before
them.[14] Ample evidence exists that other churches, like the Church
of Scotland, did supply allowances to needy members of their
congregations, with the intention of supplementing sums received
from earnings and from other charities. The necessary funds were
obtained from weekly and special collections.

Orphans presented a special problem to the parishes. Unless
some relative was willing to take the child into his home the session
had to find accommodation; even if relatives were willing to care for
the child, it was often necessary for the parish to supply some aid,
thus causing an increased burden on the funds. This was the case
even if only the father died, for a mother left with several young
children could not adequately provide for them. Such a problem had
an adverse effect on the poor's fund, as it was expensive to provide
board for the orphans.

Different criteria of need were used by different parishes as
circumstances altered. Thus in Tranent, Alexander Paterson, a long
standing pensioner, had his pension withdrawn when he married a
younger woman whose means were reputed to be sufficient to maintain

him.[15] A case from Cardross indicates that relief was denied not
because the individual was employed, but rather because his earnings
were too large; the session found that John Crawford, a labourer who
had petitioned for support from the funds, had earnings which amounted
to from 16 to 20 shillings per month, hence they felt that he was not
entitled to relief.[16] The Dalkeith heritors refused to give aid to
Hugh Adam's wife, a resident for five years, until she produced a
certificate from her former parish attesting to her sound moral
character.[17]

The northeast Lowland parishes developed a method of dividing
the poor on their rolls into classes, with each person in a class
receiving the same amount of relief. The class a recipient was
placed in depended upon his circumstances; the criteria for each
class is not known. Cawdor, Nairnshire, seems to be the first parish
to use this system by dividing the poor into three classes: four in
the first class received a half-yearly allowance of 4s., four in the
second class an allowance of 3s., and nine in the third class 2s.
each.[18] This practice quickly spread to the other northeast Lowland
parishes, with the most popular method a three class distinction. A
recipient could be moved to a different class if his conditions changed.

Pension lists were frequently restricted by establishing
either a set number of pensioners or a fixed amount of total
expenditure. This procedure was found in parishes throughout
Scotland, exhibiting little regional variation. For example, the
Cawdor session, because of inadequate funds to meet the growing
demand, agreed to limit the number on the roll at any given time
to twenty-one. No additional applicants were to be admitted until
a vacancy on the list occurred. A reserve fund was established for
meeting occasional, extraordinary distress.[19] Mr. Turcan, the
minister at Tranent, informed the heritors in 1782 that he had
disbursed to the poor £1 9s. 5d. for the current week, which was 13d.

more than the £17 Scots (28s. 4d. Sterling) weekly maximum established
in November, 1750. As the price of meal had greatly increased and the
number of applicants was growing, he asked the heritors to establish
a more realistic limit, which they agreed to do.[20]

The funds were distributed at varying periods of time. In the
northern areas common time periods were annual and semi-annual
distributions of money following the Sacraments; only in a few cases
were they made either monthly or weekly. Nevertheless, if need arose,
additional payments were made. For the other areas of Scotland the
most frequent period of payment was weekly. A few instances of
monthly payments were found; only in rare cases were the periods of
payment of a longer duration. Sometimes situations occurred as in
Elgin, where "the Session were of opinion that there should be no
general distribution to the poor at this time. But that such as
were in very nessitious [sic] circumstances might have some light
supply".[21]

No statements were found describing the method of determining
the amount of aid an individual should receive. Typically, a "...
distribution was made to the poor according to every ones necessity
as far as could be known and the subject would allow out of what
collections had been".[22] It would appear that there were no set
rules; each case was reviewed according to its own merits. Reference
was made to the available evidence, and if it later became apparent
that the situation had changed, the pension was adjusted, as in
Salton where a medical certificate was produced indicating that Mary
Lourie's health had worsened, resulting in an increased allowance.[23]
But even if a paupers' circumstances improved, his allowance was not
necessarily decreased, as illustrated by the following quotation:

> The meeting having considered William Muirhead and his
> wife's application for an addition to their weekly aliment,
> find that besides three shillings a week with a house and
> garden, coals, and medical attendance which they have from
> the Kirk Session, they receive two shillings a week from
> a Friendly Society, and as they have no children, the

> meeting are of opinion that their means of support are
> fully better than those of any other in similar circum-
> stances in the parish, and that they are even better
> provided for than many labouring men in the neighbour-
> hood who have a wife and family to support. In these
> circumstances the meeting do not feel justified in
> increasing their allowance *for the present* (Italics
> added).[24]

With the benefits they were receiving from the friendly society it is
remarkable that they were granted aid in the first instance, quite
apart from the possibility of a future increase. It should be noted
that on 11th January, 1845, William Muirhead and his wife filed an
application with the Court of Session for increased allowances, and
the heritors agreed that an attempt should be made to resist this
plea.

Besides monetary payments, most parishes gave their paupers some
additional benefit in the form of house rent, coal, clothing, or food.
Cromarty annually distributed among the poor six bolls, six and one-
half pecks of meal. Most parishes gave coal during the winter season.
Anstruther, Fife, provided clothes for the needy and set 5s. as the
maximum amount for house rent. Anstruther, after 1831, also impressed
upon individuals the need for personal cleanliness and the ventilation
of houses. The most unusual distribution was made in Elgin, where
Bibles were annually given to the poor. One wonders if they were able
to read their Bible; they would certainly be reminded that man cannot
live by bread alone.

Most parishes made provision for the education of poor children.
The funds for this purpose did not necessarily come from the general
poor's funds, but rather from mortifications given for that purpose.
In Falkirk ten or twelve poor scholars were educated by the school
master gratis, as a condition of Mr. Scott's Mortification. In
Cramond it was ordered in 1797 that poor scholars were to be given
only three years of schooling. Ayton's heritors in 1878 felt that
only children between the ages of six and ten should be sent to school,

as that was sufficient time to learn to read and write. The session
of Tranent after hearing 17 poor scholars read, decided that Peggy
Hinly should be struck from the list, as she could read fairly well.[25]

Some parishes provided medical aid, usually by reimbursing the
surgeon for his services to the poor. The parish of Salton "ordered
the Sum of five Guineas to be given to Mr. Machie, Surgeon at
Ormiston for attendance upon and drugs to the poor for about 7 years
past".[26] In Ayton, Mr. Colville, surgeon, was annually given £5 to
attend the sick paupers.[27] With the establishment of Royal
Infirmaries at Edinburgh, Aberdeen, and Glasgow, parishes in these
areas were encouraged to contribute to them, and thus obtain
privileges in sending patients. Dunoon, Argyleshire, paid £50 to the
Royal Infirmary in Glasgow.[28] These sums allowed the parish to
recommend two patients annually to each Infirmary for all time coming.
As a total of £124 was collected, there was a balance of £24, the
interest of which was used to defray the expenses of the sick poor
requiring to go to the infirmary.

Times of particularly severe economic distress placed great
hardships upon the people. One such period was the extreme shortage
of grain and meal in the northern parts of Scotland during the winter
of 1782-3, resulting from several years succession of bad harvests.
In a situation such as this the parish bought large quantities of
grain and sold it to the inhabitants at a reduced rate. The problem
during the winter of 1782-3 was so severe and on such a large scale
that the government, through the Barons of Exchequer, gave the
parishes a grant with which they could buy grain.

A perculiar practice developed in the Lowland areas in the 1750's
and rapidly spread to the remainder of Scotland; a practice not
sanctioned by the law or tested in the Court of Session. In effect
it tied the poor to the box by demanding that before they received
any assistance, a disposition had to be signed, which made the poor's

fund the recipient's heir. The amount of relief given had to be
repaid before any balance could be distributed to the pauper's
relatives. Likewise, if a pauper wished to be removed from the roll
before his death, he had to repay the parish the sums expended on him.
The extent of a pauper's liability was limited to the amount received.
The effect of this policy was to restrict the number of applications;
only those in a situation of extreme destitution were willing to sign
dispositions.

Despite the clear ruling in law that no help was to be given to
the able-bodied, there were exceptions. Cases of giving relief to
able-bodied unemployed were numerous; and instances of providing aid
to the able-bodied employed were also found.

It is curious that, at a time when it was held that relief should
be given only as a last resort and never to the able-bodied, the
following should appear: "They are of opinion that the labouring
poor in the parish who by reason of the present Extra-ordinary dearth
are reduced to poverty and want, have a Just claim to be Supported
from Said funds".[29] Similar entries were found for other parishes,
indicating that the able-bodied were supplied with relief. In a
number of parishes the recipients were also currently employed. In
Dingwall, Cromarty, a number of names on the poor's lists had
occupations appended; it is not known whether these people were still
employed, or whether it referred to their former occupation. Nonetheless, the highest pension listed on the Dingwall rolls was paid to
one of the elders - a matter which must give rise to some speculation.[30]

It is also evident that occasional relief was given to the able-
bodied during times of temporary distress, arising either from
unemployment or sickness. In such circumstances the individuals
remained on the roll only as their circumstances required relief.
Sometimes there was widespread unemployment, in which case some
parishes felt an obligation to try to aid those affected, though
assistance was not usually given from the funds. A special voluntary

subscription was the typical method of securing funds for the unemployed, but occasionally an assessment was imposed.

The amounts of relief given varied considerably between regions. (See Maps 2 and 3) On the supply side expenditure was conditioned by the available funds. The size of the fund for distribution to the poor was a direct function of the income generating capacity of the parish, together with the willingness and number of persons capable of giving. On the demand side the total amount of relief distributed was a function of the applications for assistance and the willingness of the administrators to grant relief. Both the supply of and demand for funds were influenced by the degree to which the market economy had developed. For in each society pauperism is an ascribed status, the level to a large extent depending upon the ability of the defining society to provide public relief. Such an ability cannot be entirely divorced from the degree of development of the market economy, particularly when relief is provided in the form of money allowances rather than in kind. Furthermore, the more developed an economy, the greater the reliance placed on money allowance. Also, the more developed the market economy, the greater the demand for such allowances. Therefore, *a priori*, one should expect money allowances to paupers to be greater in industrial areas than in unimproved agricultural areas.

The expenditure areas derived from the 1818 and 1839 Reports show that the Highland parishes had the lowest monetary level of expenditure per pauper in Scotland, and indeed in Britain. This is a situation not too surprising in the light of the existing conditions. The allowances in the Highlands were higher in the southern portion than the northern, and those in the eastern parts were greater than in the west. Clearly, the capacity to generate parochial funds for the poor was restricted by low money incomes. Many of the Highland landlords in the remoter areas were by this

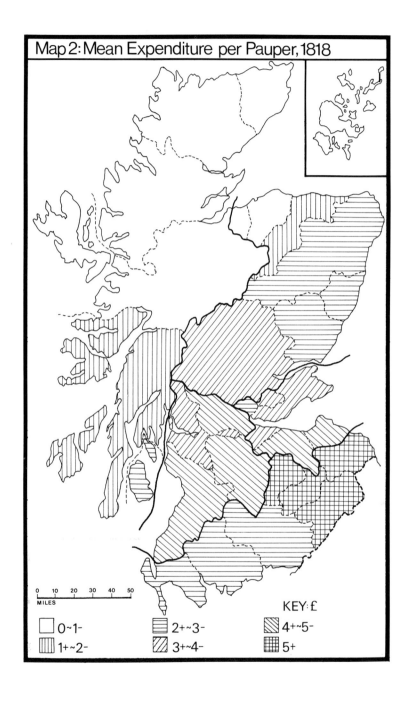

Map 2: Mean Expenditure per Pauper, 1818

KEY: £

0~1-

1+~2-

2+~3-

3+~4-

4+~5-

5+

0 10 20 30 40 50
MILES

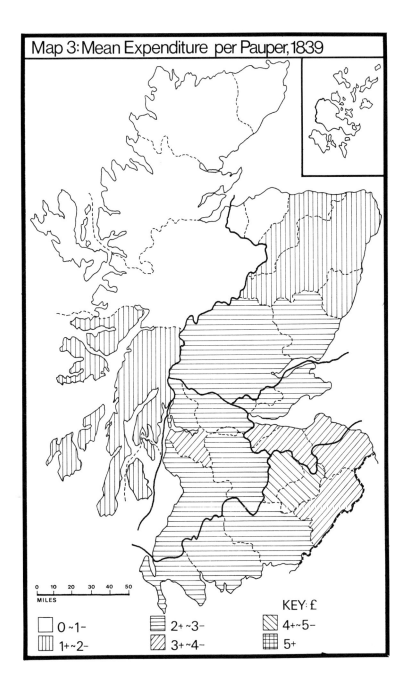

Map 3: Mean Expenditure per Pauper, 1839

MILES
0 10 20 30 40 50

KEY: £
☐ 0~1-
▥ 1+~2-
▤ 2+~3-
▧ 3+~4-
▨ 4+~5-
▦ 5+

date absentees, removed from the people and unaware of their needs, except those expressed by the tacksmen. Absenteeism also substantially reduced the proceeds of the church collections.

Factors on the demand side were also conducive in the Highlands to a low level of relief payments. Although the last remnants of the clan system were dying out, traditional attitudes probably conditioned the people not to question the policy of their chiefs or their agents, but to accept their circumstances without complaint. Besides, if the Highland ethos of self-reliance and independence was typical, perhaps the people were embarrassed in applying for an augmentation of an inadequate allowance. It would appear that in many parts of the Highlands, parishes could provide substantially below average relief payments because the inhabitants were not dependent upon money incomes: rent was often paid in kind and by labour, peat was cut for fuel, fish provided an important source of food. These were all means of providing assistance in kind which could not easily be pursued in a developed market economy. Moreover, money relief payments had to remain low in many Highland parishes because the great amount of destitution (low ability to consume) derived from a low income generating capacity and an inability to give to the church collections, thus producing scanty funds for distribution.

The expenditure aspects of the Highland scene is to be contrasted to those of the area between the Forth and the Tweed, where expenditure per pauper was the highest in Scotland, especially that in the southern district adjacent to the English border. Although the market-development hypothesis cannot provide the sole explanation for the high level of relief payments, it is possible to demonstrate that factors which were dependent on the market economy influenced the level of allowances. If, as has been suggested elsewhere,[31] there was a relatively low demand for general labourers, they would have left the area in search of employment opportunities elsewhere.

Such emigration would cause an upward shift in the age structure, diminishing the amount of support the aged received from younger relatives and friends. The net effect would be a growing demand for relief. Similar circumstances developed in the Highlands, but the crucial difference was an ability and a willingness to provide relatively high allowances from the public funds in the Forth-Tweed area.

In combination with the market-development hypothesis, an imitation of English poor relief practices can also account for the observed phenomena in the Borders. According to this argument, the paupers were aware of higher relief payments in England, and thus they demanded increased allowances as a right. This was a major conclusion of the 1818 Report. The evidence from the kirk session minutes and heritors' records, however, indicates that only individuals applied for augmentation of allowances and only as a result of a change in personal circumstances; there appears to have been no concerted appeal or demand. This theory, as stated, emphasises only the demand side and fails to allow for the possibility that it was the administrators who were the imitators. Perhaps the landlords, instead of caring for their own tenants, felt that their costs would be lower if relief was provided from the public funds, hence spreading the burden among all the assessable inhabitants of the parish.

The industrial area of the Clyde basin and agricultural parishes in near proximity was another area of relatively high expenditure per pauper. The Clyde basin was greatly dependent upon the market economy. Indeed, the structure of urban areas was not conducive to the paternal rural approach to providing relief. Allowances in rural parishes close to major urban areas were higher than in other rural areas, reflecting, perhaps, an intensive agriculture geared to meeting the demands of the urban populations. Such a situation meant high agricultural wages in order to counter the attractions of industrial employment, resulting in a higher cost of living and a need to provide relatively greater allowances. Social and economic factors changed faster in this area than in the remainder of Scotland, causing not only the amounts of relief payments to be higher, but also for them to increase over time at a faster rate.

The data of the 1818 and 1839 Reports were also evaluated with respect to the percentage of the population who were paupers. (See Maps 4 and 5.) In 1818 the percentages were above average in most of the counties in the northern areas of Scotland and in the counties adjacent to the border; that for the industrial counties and the counties in the western half of the Southern Uplands was below average. The remainder of Scotland yielded near average values. By 1839 a very complex picture had emerged. Basically, the higher relative number of paupers relieved was again in the northern regions and the Borders, though the remainder of Scotland exhibits a random mix. Average percentages for 1839 were higher than for 1818.

It should be noted that, with the exception of those in the southwestern corner of Scotland, the counties with the lowest percentage of paupers were the industrial ones. This is perhaps what one would expect given the seasonal nature of agriculture, where relatives were not able to provide a complete subsistence during the winter months. Indeed, most parish rolls exhibit a greater number of paupers during the winter than during the summer. The relative numbers relieved in parishes with advanced market economies should be less than in those where such an economy was less developed, as such aged persons who had a marginal propensity to become paupers could seek light industrial employment.

The high percentage of paupers in the western and northern Highlands can be accounted for by the collapse of the traditional forms of landownership and the economic framework. People were forced to coastal settlements where they could not always gain a

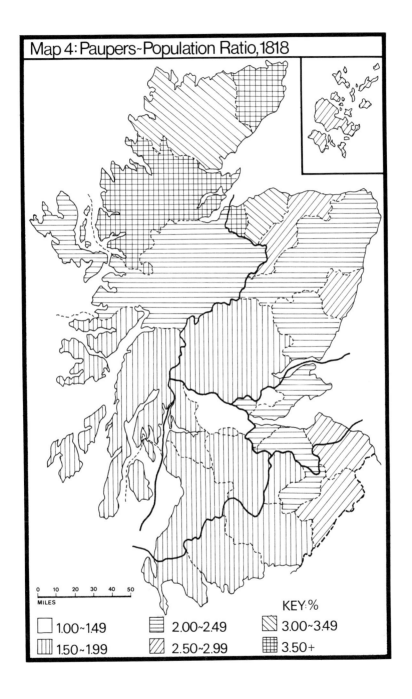

Map 4: Paupers~Population Ratio, 1818

0 10 20 30 40 50
MILES

KEY: %

☐ 1.00~1.49   ▤ 2.00~2.49   ▨ 3.00~3.49

▥ 1.50~1.99   ▨ 2.50~2.99   ▦ 3.50+

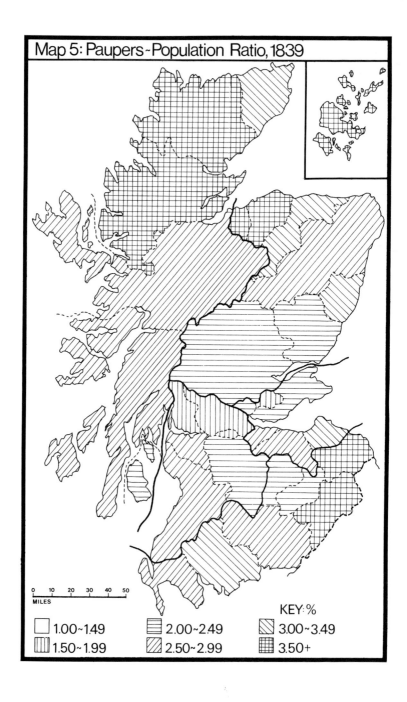

Map 5: Paupers~Population Ratio, 1839

KEY: %

1.00~1.49 2.00~2.49 3.00~3.49
1.50~1.99 2.50~2.99 3.50+

0 10 20 30 40 50
MILES

means of livelihood, indeed serious over-crowding was a major social problem. The traditional relationships between the people and the landlords and that amongst the people had broken down.[32] The amount of destitution was so great that the inhabitants were unable to help each other. The high percentage of paupers in the Borders perhaps was a reflection of general labourers leaving the area in search of employment, resulting in an upward shift in the age structure of the population, therefore causing an artificially high level of pauperism. Or, possibly the influence of the English system was being felt, the level of pauperism being defined more generously.

In most of the sample parishes the number of paupers remained at a remarkably constant level, but with considerable short term fluctuations. The upper level represents a decision by the sessions to limit absolutely the number on the roll, sometimes for decades, in other words a problem of allocating scarce resources. The lower level perhaps represents the biological minimum percentage of population falling into the categories eligible for relief, a level which increased as population increased. Fluctuations between the two levels can be accounted for by the deaths of paupers (decrease) or by deaths of persons upon whom the eligible categories were dependent (increase) or by orphans becoming too old to be eligible for relief (decrease). These first two factors, in significant numbers, were caused by unusual conditions such as famines or epidemics.

The data on the number of paupers relieved exhibit considerable annual fluctuation, with no apparent pattern emerging between the regions. Thus, it would seem reasonable to conclude that seasonal variations can be explained by local conditions. There does appear to be a tendency in the sample parishes for the number on the roll to increase both during periods of diminishing population growth rates and when there was an absolute fall in population; numbers on

the roll were either stable, or decreased during periods of substantial increases in population.

D. *Parish of Settlement and Liability*

The law stated that the parish of residence was responsible for
maintaining a pauper. The two most common means of determining the
parish of residence was either by birth or by continuous habitation
for at least three years without receiving public assistance. When
a woman married, she assumed her husband's parish as her parish of
residence. The parish for a legitimate child was his father's, and
for an illegitimate child it was his mother's. All the parishes
examined accepted these conditions, but in the case of applicants
born outside the parish, the administrators made every attempt, often
involving great expenditure of effort, to prove that the liability
for relief lay with another parish. The kirk session minutes
contained numerous examples of parishes writing to one another trying
to avoid liability, but eventually the right of the applicant to
relief was seldom denied. This was particularly the case as it was
not always possible to determine which parish should be liable.

One characteristic of the system peculiar to the Lowlands was
the removal of poor strangers before they could establish the
necessary three year's residence. The Scottish poor law made no
provision for removal, and no evidence has been found that any other
law passed by the Scottish Parliament permitted removal, thus
suggesting the existence of local rulings passed by the sheriffs.
Evidence of such rulings was found in Cardross when the individuals
hired to rid the parish of beggars and stranger poor were ordered to
"... observe and comply with the injunctions of the Proclamation by
the Sheriff and Magistrates of the County of Dumbarton".[33] It appears
that the poor law had been circumvented by demanding from strangers
settling in a parish a certificate issued by their former parish

attesting to their moral character and signifying a means of support. It must be stressed that parishes undertook to remove poor persons to prevent an additional burden of the poor's fund. They had no authority to do this from the poor law; the provisions of the Act of 1574 enabled poor people to request travel passes to their parish of residence. Some parishes found themselves located on the roads to the industrial centres and thus were plagued by paupers travelling with passes which were issued by another parish in order that the pauper could travel to his parish of residence; any parish along the way was to provide provisions and transportation through its territory.

E. Conclusions

A striking characteristic of the Scottish poor law as administered in rural parishes was its unification within what was really a slender legal framework. Despite legal provisions for independent management by the numerous parishes, there existed a surprising uniformity in practice, since innovations in policy by one rural parish spread rapidly among the others.

The law was enforced more actively in southern Scotland than in the north. The lack of a formal administrative framework in the northern regions relative to that of the southern Lowlands should not be too surprising given the remoteness and isolation of the parishes and the high degree of absenteeism. The management in the northern parishes remained voluntary, whereas the introduction of legal assessments in the south brought in salaried personnel in the form of stent collectors and overseers. These individuals, however, only carried out the wishes of the sessions and heritors.

Poor rates and expenditure in Scotland never reached the same levels as in England. The interests of the elders and heritors were often conflicting, which served to keep the rates low. The ministers and elders represented the compassionate element of administration, concerned with the moral and material well-being of the inhabitants. As the examples from the session minutes illustrate, they were liberal in the granting of relief to legitimate cases. The heritors, however, held ultimate control of the purse-strings. As principle taxpayers, they desired to keep outlays to a minimum, becoming extremely active in administration with the threat of a legal assessment. The heritors' attitudes in combination with increasing absenteeism and a lack of adequate church accommodation caused parishes to suffer from a shortage of funds.

The moral circumstances of all applicants for relief were considered before the granting of an allowance. In all cases the amount of relief granted was not sufficient to provide the sole means of livelihood: great stress was placed upon the charity of friends and relatives. Furthermore, no fixed standard was established setting the amount of the allowance, rather each case was examined according to its merits. Although contemporaries argued that moral attitudes were more strictly adhered to in the Highlands, no evidence exists to confirm this impression.

In all areas the data indicate that relief was given not only to the impotent, but also to the able-bodied during periods of temporary distress, except unemployment. Few parishes made provision for medical relief. The extent to which a parish was willing to help appears to have been a direct function of the availability of funds. All the parishes viewed the granting of relief as a loan, as the paupers were tied to the box with the signing of dispositions to their goods. Only in the parishes between the Forth and the Tweed was evidence found that the paupers were gainfully employed as a requirement for receiving relief.

The system of poor relief in rural Scotland was certainly paternal in nature. Generally the elders were sympathetic with the poors' problems, coping with the difficult question of allocating

scarce resources. The evidence indicates that the system operated
smoothly within the context of rural Scotland: the poor accepted
their lot.

---

1.   Cranstoun Kirk Session Minutes, 10th December, 1827.

2.   Croy Kirk Session Minutes, 15th August, 1771.

3.   Sorn Heritors' Records, 29th July, 1830.

4.   Fordoun Kirk Session Minutes, 10th October, 1782.

5.   Newbattle Kirk Session Minutes, 3rd September, 1812.

6.   Cromarty Kirk Session Minutes, 7th September, 1790.

7.   Canisbay Kirk Session Minutes, 9th September, 1754.

8.   Falkirk Kirk Session Minutes, 6th October, 1845.

9.   Croy Kirk Session Minutes, 4th May, 1775.

10.   Grange Kirk Session Minutes, 25th December, 1842.

11.   Kemnay Kirk Session Minutes, 31st July, 1800.

12.   Tough Kirk Session Minutes, 24th March, 1800.

13.   Grange Kirk Session Minutes, 8th September, 1782.

14.   Govan Heritors' Records, 15th August, 1816.

15.   Tranent Kirk Session Minutes, 26th April, 1768.

16.   Cardross Kirk Session Minutes, 29th May, 1831.

17.   Dalkeith Heritors' Records, 29th September, 1764.

18.   Cawdor Kirk Session Minutes, 19th January, 1773.

19.   Cawdor Kirk Session Minutes, 7th August 1775.

20.   Tranent Kirk Session Minutes, 11th November, 1782.

21.   Elgin Kirk Session Minutes, 6th May, 1768.

22.   Sorn Kirk Session Minutes, 5th August, 1753.

23.   Salton Kirk Session Minutes, 1st November, 1834.

24.   Salton Heritors' Records, 6th December, 1844.

25.   Tranent Kirk Session Minutes, 8th May, 1786.

26.   Salton Kirk Session Minutes, 15th May, 1771.

27.   Ayton Heritors' Records, 8th January, 1836.

28. Dunoon Kirk Session Minutes, 22nd April, 1813 and 2nd June, 1813.

29. Orwell Heritors' Records, 21st February, 1800.

30. Dingwall Kirk Session Minutes, 1st December, 1841.

31. Valerie Morgan, "Agricultural Wage Rates in late Eighteenth-Century Scotland", in *EcHR*, second series, vol. XXIV, 1971, p. 186.

32. T. C. Smout, *A History of the Scottish People, 1560-1830*, pp. 334-6.

33. Cardross Heritors' Records, 20th February, 1832.

CHAPTER 3: POOR RELIEF ADMINISTRATION IN URBAN SCOTLAND

The study of poor relief in urban Scotland prior to 1845 is one of similarities and contrasts, particularly between the two major burghs, Glasgow and Edinburgh. Scots law clearly established a framework within which the administration of urban relief was to operate; yet, the structure was flexible enough to enable the burghs to establish systems suitable to their own needs and desires. What was this framework, and how did practise coincide with it? Moreover, what were the policy variations between the major burghs, and how did such differences develop during the period under consideration? To answer these and other questions, several Scottish burghs have been studied in great detail, with Glasgow, Edinburgh, and Paisley yielding the most comprehensive records.

The inhabitants of Scotland's major towns, Glasgow and Edinburgh, were among the leaders of British industrial growth; moreover, the Glasgow-Edinburgh belt was the first area in Scotland to experience the impact of industrialisation. Indeed, Glasgow ranked high among British cities in the intensity of that experience. Glasgow's population nearly doubled between 1801 (77,385) and 1821 (147,043) and again by 1841 (274,324); Edinburgh's population more than doubled between 1801 (67,288) and 1841 (138,182). The spectacular rate of population growth for Glasgow can be attributed largely to the influx of Highlanders and the Irish, both groups seeking industrial employment. This phenomenal growth created pressures which caused a concentration of destitution, especially as industrial workers were extremely susceptible to variations in economic activity. Because of the increasing pressures caused by rapid urbanisation, it is not surprising to find Glasgow and Edinburgh developing new techniques of urban poor relief administration. Each city was confronted with a complex traditional system, yet each adapted the existing framework to meet the new challenges. Not surprisingly, as each city faced different

problems, the system of poor relief which evolved in each was
distinct.

Prior to 1730 the burghs studied were so small that poor relief
administration in them could not be distinguished from that in the
rural parishes as the magistrates and town councils of the burghs
usually delegated their administrative responsibilities to the
Church. But as the population of the burghs increased and became
more dense, the Church as administrator was either replaced or
supplemented by elected lay officials. The first clear move
separating rural and urban administration was made in Glasgow in
1731, with the founding of the Town's Hospital, a workhouse.

Prior to 1731 poor relief in Glasgow was administered by four
groups: the Town Council, the General Session of the Church for
Glasgow, the Incorporated Trades (the producers' guild), and the
Merchants' House (the merchants' guild). Each of these worked
independently, administering relief mainly to their own members.
Under this framework an effective unified system of relief was
impossible. Although by law the magistrates and town council were
responsible for the administration of poor relief within their
bounds, it appears that, by and large, they accepted responsibility
only for the residue of pauperism. The situation came to a head in
1731, when, because of increasing problems of destitution and
begging in Glasgow, the magistrates and town council consulted the
other groups providing assistance. Their object was to develop a
new system of poor relief in Glasgow. Their efforts resulted in
the creation in 1731 of the Town's Hospital to house and employ
profitably poor indigent children, old deranged men and women, and
others rendered unable to provide for themselves. There were now
two institutions for supplying relief in Glasgow, the new Hospital
and the General Session. These two organisations administered their
respective funds independently of each other, though persons could

not gain admission to the Town's Hospital without being referred by
their individual parish kirk session.

The Glasgow General Session was a policy formulating organisation
composed of the minister and elders from each of the parishes within
the Royalty of Glasgow. As was the general rule in Scotland, each
parish was divided into 'portions', with an elder responsible for
its poor assigned to each. Persons first applied for assistance to
their elder, who gave the applicant temporary aid while investigating
his claim. The elder did this by determining the applicant's need,
and whether he had been an industrious resident of the burgh of Glasgow
for at least three years. If these conditions were met, the applicant
was placed upon the session rolls and received a monthly allowance, of
which there were thirteen payments during the year. He remained on the
session rolls until the maximum amount which the session could give
was insufficient to maintain him; he was then transferred to the rolls
of the Town's Hospital, his name being removed from the session's rolls.
The sessions' funds were derived from church door collections,
proclamation fees, mortcloth dues, fines for irregular marriages and
births, and donations. Each session, until 1821, paid the General
Session one-half of its collections. The General Session then
distributed the funds to the parishes in proportion to the number of
poor on their rolls.

The Town's Hospital was managed by a group of forty-eight
directors and the Lord Provost. Twelve directors were elected by
the town council (six of whom were magistrates), twelve by the
General Session (including four ministers in rotation), twelve by the
Merchants' House (including the Dean of Guild), and twelve by the
Incorporated Trades (including the Convenor). Hence, all the groups
providing relief prior to 1731 were equally represented in the new
system, and any change in the Hospital rules and regulations had to
be ratified by three of the four electing societies. Quarterly

meetings were held in February, May, August, November, with any twenty-
five directors constituting a quorum. From the forty-eight directors
a Weekly Committee of eight was elected, each society choosing two.
This Committee met in the Hospital every Tuesday to administer the
orders of the directors. It was also responsible for handling the
admission of the poor and the daily business. Each director had the
power to order beggars into the Hospital. Besides the directors, who
freely provided their services, there were a number of paid servants:
an overseer, a school-master, several nurses, a cook, and a surgeon.

A change in Glasgow from the system as above described can be
dated from 23rd April, 1818, when the directors of the Hospital
appointed a Committee to examine the system of poor relief
management. The Committee's report dealt with the proper recipients
of relief besides recommending several administrative changes.[1]
First, it was agreed that by 1819 all out-pensions would be paid in
money instead of meal, indicating that the attempt to prevent the
exchanging of meal for other goods, particularly alcohol, had failed.
The Committee also felt that the practice of giving meal was too
inconvenient. For example on one Saturday, 3802 pounds of meal were
distributed among 512 paupers - 201 received six pounds each, 276
received eight pounds each, ten pounds each was given to 16 persons,
and 19 received twelve pounds each. The meal was given out by the
Hospital inmates, who were not supervised, and there was no check on
the quantity distributed. The Committee estimated that the expense
of giving meal was fifty per cent more than if money had been paid.
Second, it was decided to end the practice of having boarders,
individuals who paid from eighteen pounds to twenty pounds per year
to live in the Hospital, but who did not have to follow the rules.
Third, there was the case of the children. The Hospital had
responsibility for three classes of these: (1) orphans - children
who either had no parent or had been deserted and were at the age of

education; (2) exposed children - foundlings given out to nurse until six or seven years of age and kept on the funds until the age of ten for boys and eleven for girls, and then apprenticed; and (3) adopted children - those admitted as infants with a payment of thirty pounds, no questions asked. This last formula perhaps reflected on the morality of the upper classes, for few others could afford a thirty pound payment. The practice of keeping adopted children was begun in 1802, and, as the mortality of such children was high, was considered as a source of revenue. Indeed, a profit of one thousand, two hundred pounds was derived from this category between 1802 and 1818. Nonetheless, it was decided to discontinue the acceptance of adopted children. (This practice, however, was reinstated in 1823.) More generally, it was decided that children should no longer be kept in the Hospital, but rather be boarded out in the country, as they would only tend to learn listless and idle habits from intercourse with the aged, yet hardened sinner.

These changes, though important, were but a prelude to what was to follow. With the inception of St. John's Church on 29th September, 1819, the break-down of the old system was accelerated. The St. John's experiment under the leadership of the Rev. Dr. Thomas Chalmers has been the subject of much admiration in poor law history and is often cited as an important case study in how the problems of poverty can be solved by a formula of self-help. Briefly, at St. John's Chalmers attempted to care for the parish's poor without relying on the public legal funds. Chalmers divorced himself from the established poor relief administration in Glasgow and went his own way, creating a system of chaos, deception, and misgivings.[2]

The General Session twice submitted its resignation in protest of Chalmer's work, the final time being 1st February, 1821. From that day on each session dealt individually with the Town's Hospital. Though individuals continued to apply to their elder for poor relief and were placed first on the session's rolls, the old system had ended. The major change in management was that the individual sessions no longer gave their collections to the General Session to be distributed to the parishes according to their proportion of paupers. Each parish session administered its own funds, any surplus of revenue over expenditure being retained. If a session's funds, consisting of the church door collections, were not adequate, it drew from the Hospital's funds, which were composed primarily of the revenue from the assessment.

In the Edinburgh area there developed starting in 1740, a system of workhouses designed after the Glasgow Town's Hospital. Unlike Glasgow, where the adjacent densely populated parishes of Govan, Gorbals and Barony administered relief as rural parishes, in the Edinburgh area the rural (suburban) parishes of Canongate and St. Cuthbert's imitated the administrative practices of the Royalty. It is remarkable that the three Edinburgh area parishes acted independently of each other, with little hint of co-operation. This was perhaps the most significant characteristic of poor relief administration in the Edinburgh area. Indeed, the poor often took advantage of the confused state of the administration by simultaneously being on the rolls of all three parishes.

On 23rd February, 1740, the Lord Provost, magistrates and town council of Edinburgh signed a contract with the General Kirk Session delegating the whole management of the City's poor to a group of ninety-six men (eventually the number was extended to 108 with the establishment of several different parishes) elected annually from the groups administering some type of relief and the groups carrying great political influence. The 96 general managers met quarterly to determine the policy of the workhouse. The terms of the contract of agreement could be terminated only by the kirk sessions, either individually or as a group. The business of the Edinburgh Charity

Workhouse was managed by the weekly committee, consisting of fifteen men elected from the ranks of the general managers. They were divided into three five-man classes, and each week one class was responsible for visiting the House daily, except Sunday and Tuesday. All fifteen men met every Tuesday at 3.00 to inspect the management of the House and the behaviour of the residents, to issue warrants upon the persons entrusted with the funds, and to make payments to the out-pensioners.

Workhouses were established in the parishes of Canongate and St. Cuthbert's, the managerial set-up similar to that of Edinburgh. Hence, within the Edinburgh area the town council in the Royalty and the Church in the parishes of Canongate and St. Cuthbert's delegated their responsibilities toward the poor. The workhouse managers were the sole administrators of the public poor relief funds, deciding on all applications for public assistance within their respective areas.

A new system of management was adopted in St. Cuthbert's in 1833, under which 120 men were elected solely by the heritors (60) and the kirk session (60). The managers were divided into six divisions of twenty each, besides the following six special committees: Finance, Out-pension, House, Assessment, Education and Kirk-Session. The last committee was necessary because the session refused to take part in the management as a result of a dispute over who should receive the proceeds from the graveyard. Individuals applied to the manager of their district for relief; if a recipient moved from one district to another within St. Cuthbert's he was struck off the lists and had to re-apply in his new district.

Several attempts were made to unify the system of poor relief administration within the Edinburgh area. In 1747 St. Cuthbert's session suggested that their poor should be housed in the Edinburgh Charity Workhouse with the managers of that institution controlling the funds; this was again proposed in 1755, but neither suggestion was adopted. In 1754 the session argued that the City should help to provide for the poor in the suburbs, as no distinction could logically be made as to parish, particularly as many people lived in St. Cuthbert's but worked in the City. In 1749 the Edinburgh town council petitioned parliament for an act combining into one unit for the purposes of poor relief Edinburgh, Canongate, St. Cuthbert's, North and South Leith. The poor's rate would be levied over the whole area by trustees appointed by parliament, these trustees would manage the Edinburgh Charity Workhouse, which would house all the poor. Even though the kirk sessions agreed with the proposal, it was dropped, as the trades, heritors, and faculty of the College of Justice did not agree.

Initially, in all of the burghs examined the funds for poor relief were derived from voluntary sources. The various Church sessions used one-half of their church door collections, proclamation of marriage fees, mortcloth dues, fines for irregular marriages and births, and donations. The funds for the various workhouses were derived from annual contributions from the various societies comprising the management and from sale of work undertaken by the inhabitants of the houses. In all the burghs examined church door collections from Church of Scotland churches comprised the major component of the voluntary sources of funds. As the population of the towns, and particularly Glasgow, increased, church accommodation failed to increase at the same rate. The resultant was that church door collections per capita fell. Such collections quickly proved to be insufficient as a major source of funds, and it became necessary for all burghs to impose a legal assessment on their inhabitants. The problem was intensified because of dissenting groups; in Scotland dissenters are members of all non-Church of Scotland churches. In Glasgow in 1836, forty-two per cent of the population were dissenters. This percentage was increased with the Disruption in 1843, when over one-half of the members of the Established Church left and formed the Free Church.

In Glasgow the first year in which a legal assessment in aid of
Hospital funds was regularly imposed was 1774. It was levied on the
inhabitants by valuation of heritable and of personal property,
according to the individual's wealth, circumstances, and ability.
The levy was made by fifteen men chosen annually by the magistrates
and town council, but not of their number. The following procedure
was used to establish the amount of the assessment: the directors
of the Hospital determined the amount of funds needed in excess of
the contributions from the various societies, sent a request for
this amount to the town council, which, after agreement, issued an
order for an assessment to be levied for the desired amount. Once
the amount of the assessment was known, the fifteen member committee
determined the value of each inhabitant whose total worth was greater
than three hundred pounds, and after the total valuation was known,
the rate of valuation was determined in order to raise the necessary
assessment.

No indication of complaints against the mode of assessment in
Glasgow has been found until 1820, when the town council appointed
a committee to consider changing the mode to rental value. After
much debate the council was pressured to drop the matter. All was
quiet until 1833, when an article appeared in the *Scots Times*
complaining that the mode of assessment on means and substance was
offensive, inquisitorial, unjust, and oppressive, that the fifteen
men determining the means of the inhabitants did so with reference
to their style of living, number of visitors, kind of business and
trade, and possession of heritable property, and that the committee
members often used the information for personal gain. This was
followed by another article opposing a change in the mode to
valuation of rental because under it the wealthy would not be paying
their proper share, although tenants would find themselves faced

with a new tax. The matter came to a close in 1835, when the town
council's decision to propose introducing a bill to parliament to
lower the taxable amount of means and substance to one hundred
pounds was not carried through.

From its inception in 1740 the Edinburgh Charity Workhouse was
besieged with financial difficulties. Besides trouble in raising
enough funds to pay for construction of the buildings, the managers
had problems obtaining the necessary amounts for the daily operation
of the House. The problem was intensified when it was discovered
that church collections were not yielding the expected one thousand
seven hundred pounds per annum. By 1765 the House was in debt for
about five hundred pounds, causing the managers to appeal to the
town council for help and receiving it in the form of grants. The
first really serious financial difficulties for the Edinburgh
Workhouse arose in the 1770s, when the managers approached the town
council about their debt of three hundred pounds, besides a considerable sum due for meal, malt and flour. Discussion followed on the
best method of relieving the situation; possible solutions mentioned
were to increase the assessment, to impose a voluntary collection,
to appeal for subscriptions, to obtain further grants from the town
council, or to borrow from the banks. The last solution was adopted
and the town council gave their approval to borrow six hundred
pounds from the Royal Bank in order to pay off the debt. This was
the first of a long series of such transactions. These crises arose
primarily because of increased numbers of poor due to war, increased
cos⁺ of provisions, the inability of the stent masters to collect the
assessment in the year it was due, and the fact that the managers
received funds from the assessment independently of their needs, as
the assessment was always a fixed rate of two per cent of rental
value. By 1812, however, the situation was so acute that the rate
of assessment was increased to three per cent, where it remained

until 1822, when it was increased to three and a half per cent and
eventually reached seven per cent.

Bad as these financial difficulties were, they were insignificant
compared with the troubles arising from the town council. In May
1809 parliament passed a Bill annexing a portion of St. Cuthbert's
to Edinburgh. In order to compensate the parish of St. Cuthbert's
for funds which would be lost, the town council was forced to pay
St. Cuthbert's three hundred pounds annually, to be paid from the
poor's fund. The Workhouse managers predicted financial ruin if
the town council demanded payment out of the poor's fund, resulting
in the council's agreeing not to press for payment. Suddenly, on
22nd February, 1821, the town council demanded payment of the debt;
the principal amounted to £4,500 and the interest was £1819 18s. 9d.,
a total of £6319 18s. 9d. The debt increased annually thereafter,
with a substantial increase in 1832, due to the cholera epidemic.
In 1827 the managers borrowed upon the "*security* of the *arrears of
assessment*, and the *current assessment* for the year". This practice
was carried on until 1832, when the debt amounted to £15,876 and
arrears of assessment for £14,693. Prior to this date the City
collected the assessment, the managers having no control, nor were
they allowed to examine the books of the collector. In 1832 they
finally got control of the collections and discovered that the
arrears were only one-quarter of their stated value, resulting in
the creditors' refusing any more advancements, and the managers being
forced to buy all goods with ready cash. All attempts to get the
town council to increase the assessment proved futile. Because of
the town council's unwillingness to co-operate the Workhouse
managers resigned at a meeting held on 8th October, 1840, pointing
out that by law the town council was solely responsible for the
poor, and the fact that they delegated their powers to the managers
did not relieve them of the responsibility of paying the debt.

Although in each burgh examined there was no exact description of those eligible to receive relief, it is clear that assistance was extended to orphans under the age of fourteen, the aged and the impotent. Except for inmates of the workhouses, the amount of the allowance was not sufficient to provide the sole means of support. The matter of extending public relief to the able-bodied is not so clear cut. In all the burghs workhouses were established as a 'means test', as it was impossible in a town to know everyone or to distinguish between 'good' and 'bad' claims in any other way. Even when the workhouses made a provision for out-pensioners, relief was granted only if the applicant was willing to enter the workhouse. Furthermore, the recipient of relief was 'tied-to-the-box', as inmates upon entering the workhouse had to turn over their goods and out-pensioners had to sign a disposition giving the workhouse a claim on the value of their possessions in the amount of relief granted.

In Glasgow the managers of the Town's Hospital recognised that the City's poor had a *right* to be relieved. Prior to 1774 all paupers on the rolls of the Town's Hospital were inmates of the Hospital, their allowance the common provision of that institution of clothes, linen, and food. The out-pensioners of the sessions were given monthly money allowances. When the Hospital started admitting out-pensioners to its roll in 1774, because of a lack of accommodation in the Hospital, all its out-pensioners were paid by a monthly allotment of meal, but the sessions continued giving money allowances: by 1818 the sessions allowed from 1s. 6d. to 4s. 6d. per month, and if, because of bad health, this supply was insufficient, the Weekly Committee of the Hospital allowed an additional 5s. to 10s. in temporary aid. For a permanent case if the session's allowance was not sufficient, the pauper was placed on the out-pension roll of the Hospital and paid in either meal or money; if money, the person received from 5s. to 10s. per month, or in extreme cases 15s. per month; if payment was in the form of meal, he received from twenty-four to forty-eight pounds weekly. In times of great distress additional allowances were provided.

From its inception the managers of the Edinburgh Charity Workhouse provided out-door relief: if an elderly person could be cared for better in his own home, he was given relief as an out-pensioner; poor criminals were housed in the Correction House at the expense of the managers; orphans above two years of age were housed in the Orphans Hospital, and infant children were bound out to wet nurse, with the surgeon's advice, for at least two years; pauper lunatics were housed in cells at Bedlam.

In order to gain an understanding of the circumstances in which applicants were accepted upon the funds of the Canongate Charity Workhouse, a number of entries will be given from the managers' minutes illustrating the action taken on petitions. On 19th October, 1762, Widow Tervy, aged 74, was given 5d. per week out-pension, as all the beds were full. On 30th November, 1762, Ann Bennett was denied access to the House, because the physician stated she was "in distress and unfit to be received in House"; she was given 4d. per week as an out-pensioner. On 1st March, 1763, Bell Sharp, age 5, was admitted to the House on the condition that her uncle pay 40s. per year support, as she was not a resident of Canongate. On 14th August, 1764, Margaret Cowan was denied relief, as she had been a beggar. On 15th April, 1766, the managers allowed James Mason, a resident for three years, a quarter's wet nurse for one of his new-born triplets, since he had other children to support; relief was granted because he was known to be a very 'industrious' man. On 18th April, 1775, Isobel Grahame was denied an out-pension, because she refused entry to the House. On 5th July, 1803, it was ordered that no person of unsound state of mind be admitted into the House. From these and

thousands of other entries, the impression emerges that the managers
at Canongate were only too willing to provide relief; the only
reason for which relief was continually denied was that of bad
character. A surprising number of persons, however, were re-admitted
to the House after being struck off the rolls. A case in point was
Mrs Napier, who was expelled from the House for drinking on 20th
September, 1762. After petitioning she was re-admitted on 21st
September on the grounds that if she drank again she would be
expelled forever. But Mrs Napier was perennially expelled on
drinking charges and re-admitted, until she got mad at the managers
and moved to London, never to be heard of again. One wonders how
she fared in London under the English poor law.

The managers of St. Cuthbert's Charity Workhouse were probably
more stringent about giving relief than were the other workhouses,
as a very high proportion of the petitions were denied relief. In
1771 the managers, after examining Widow Baxter's situation, "appoint
her to take out her son and appoint a foot chain and a pair of hand-
cuffs to be made for him and allow her to apply when in straits".
Relief was denied to an orphan girl, age 10, as she was found to be
old enough to fend for herself.

Usually, the St. Cuthbert's managers were willing to admit
healthy children, as they could be turned into a source of revenue
by binding them out as apprentices, particularly after 1790, when
David Dale asked the Edinburgh Charity Workhouse for children to
employ in his cotton mill; as the Edinburgh Workhouse was unable to
supply a sufficient number, the St. Cuthbert's managers asked the
House master to approach Mr Dale, resulting in Dale's promising to
clothe and feed the children and provide them with jobs after their
indentures expired, if the period of indenture was either five or
six years. The managers agreed to these proposals after Dale
promised to provide the children with an education. The House

initially sent thirty-one boys and eleven girls. On 4th August, 1801,
complaints were received that the *managers* at New Lanark had not
followed the agreements of the indentures, hence it was agreed to
send the children to Blantyre, especially as New Lanark wanted all
children for seven years and Blantyre wanted the children from four to
six years, with none under the age of nine being bound.[3]

With respect to the granting of relief to the able-bodied most
burghs were willing to provide some form of assistance during periods
of temporary distress; the source of funds for such relief was either
public funds or special voluntary subscriptions. Such relief was
given to both the able-bodied employed and the able-bodied unemployed.
In Glasgow the unemployed generally were relieved from funds raised
by special voluntary subscriptions; but both the sessions and the
Town's Hospital were providing them with assistance from the public
funds from at least 1808. Surprisingly the directors of the Hospital
in 1841 even stated that the able-bodied unemployed had a *right* to
relief.

In Canongate all cases of extraordinary pensioners (individuals
needing only temporary assistance and not legally entitled to relief)
were supposedly handled by the kirk session, but this was not always
the case. For example, the managers gave to Andrew Hutchison, an
able-bodied unemployed individual with a wife and three children,
1s. per week, with relief to continue at the managers' pleasure. In
1765 John Flemming was given 8d. per week because his wife was sick
and unable to care for his four children; Mr Flemming was currently
employed. Other forms of relief to able-bodied employed individuals
were to accept one or two of their children into the House during
times of distress, or to allow the Trades to house their members in
the House.

The burgh of Paisley provides an excellent case study in the
handling of relief to the able-bodied during periods of large scale

unemployment, though the methods cannot be considered typical of the Scottish experience, as the other burghs did not face such acute problems with unemployment. Paisley had a workhouse which provided in-door relief and out-pensions to paupers not belonging to the Church of Scotland; the general kirk session provided out-pensions to its members.

It is clear that the general kirk session was handling the main burden of dealing with the unemployed and that they faced financial difficulties, for in 1819 the directors of the Hospital [workhouse] received a directive from the magistrates to pay the kirk session three hundred pounds from the assessment to help alleviate the pressures on the session. In 1826 it was decided that the best way to provide for the unemployed operatives would be for the elders to "afford assistance in their usual way to the necessitous for which purpose funds would be furnished to them by the directors of the Hospital". Indeed, the funds were provided by a special supplementary legal assessment! This is the only known instance in a burgh of a legal assessment being levied for the sole purpose of assisting the able-bodied unemployed; the only other case of a legal assessment to assist the able-bodied occurred in 1802 in the rural parish of Dunse, which was the central issue in the famous Pollock-Darling case in which the Court of Session ruled that the able-bodied unemployed had a right to receive public relief. The assessment in Paisley in 1826 appears, however, to be unique, as no other occurred.

During the intense unemployment period in the early 1840's, the burden was shifted to private charity and two organisations were formed, the Paisley Relief Committee, which received substantial funds from the Manufacturing Relief Committee of London, and the Manufacturing Committee of Paisley, which received nine thousand pounds from local subscriptions and in 1841 provided assistance to

912 of the 2,588 unemployed weavers. Both Committees stated that
"Labour has been required from the able-bodied of the men in return
for the relief given, and the species of work was the breaking of
stones for road metal, and repairing a towing-path on the bank of
the river Cart, and some smaller jobs of similar descriptions".[4]
By March, 1842 the Paisley Relief Committee had received subscriptions
amounting to £19,633 19s. 3½d. and had provided relief to 14,791
individuals (1,518 married males, 578 unmarried males and widowers
with 5,240 dependents; 2,485 widows, deserted wives and single
females with 4,979 dependents).[5]

The best and most comprehensive data for Scotland's burghs were
obtained for Glasgow and Edinburgh. Data for the other burghs were
nearly non-existent or of limited use. As a result, the following
discussion will be centred on Glasgow and Edinburgh, and an attempt
will be made to explain the rather striking differences which emerge
between the two towns. In order to help to set the scene the
following table compares the population of the Royalties of Glasgow
and Edinburgh for census years:

Year	Glasgow		Edinburgh	
1801	46,779	(77,385)	32,975	(67,288)
1811	58,334	(100,749)	36,259	(82,624)
1821	72,765	(147,043)	51,968	(112,235)
1831	89,847	(202,426)	55,339	(136,301)
1841	120,183	(274,324)	56,330	(138,182)

NOTE: The amount in the parenthesis for Glasgow include
the Barony and Gorbals, and for Edinburgh include
Canongate and St. Cuthbert's.

As can be seen, the population of the Royalty of Glasgow was
greater than Edinburgh's by 1801 and by 1841 was more than double.
It would seem reasonable to expect, therefore, that both the absolute
extent of pauperism and the total expenditure on paupers in Glasgow
were greater than in Edinburgh.

It is possible to obtain a comparative view of the Glasgow
Town's Hospital and the Edinburgh Charity Workhouse for the years
1791-1817, the only period with data conducive to comparison.
[See Table II]. Concentrating on the number of paupers on the rolls
of each institution, several facts emerge. First, though the number
of observations for Edinburgh is limited, the Glasgow Town's Hospital
placed greater emphasis on out-pensioners than on inmates, whereas
Edinburgh stressed the granting of in-door relief. Second, the
total number relieved in Glasgow was greater than in Edinburgh, the
difference being nearly in the same proportion as the difference in
population between the two cities. This is a rather over-simplified
view, however, as unlike Edinburgh, Glasgow also had sessional rolls.
The total number of out-pensioners on session rolls was approximately
the same as the number of out-pensioners on the rolls of the Town's
Hospital. Thus, the extent of pauperism in Glasgow was proportionally
greater by a substantial amount, than in Edinburgh.

In both Glasgow and Edinburgh there were annual fluctuations in
the number of paupers on the rolls, though the pattern for each town
varied due to differing local conditions. In both cases changes in
the number of out-pensioners were more dramatic than those for the
number of inmates. This phenomenon reflects the fixed capacity of
the facilities for housing paupers and the practice that only the
"hard-core" cases were granted in-door relief. Sharp increases in
the numbers of out-pensioners represent the need to supply assistance
to marginal cases during periods of unusual stress. For example in
Glasgow the rise in the number of out-pensioners from 728 in 1800 to
1128 in 1802 was a result of the increase in grain prices due to the
scarcity of grain in 1801-2; the rise from 969 in 1811 to 1409 in
1814 and the continuance at a high level can be attributed to the
additional stresses placed on the economy by the War of 1812 with
the United States of America and also the fever epidemic and the

TABLE II: Comparative View of Glasgow Town's Hospital and Edinburgh Charity Workhouse, 1791–1817, number of inmates, total expenditure on inmates, average expenditure per inmate, number of out-pensioners, total expenditure on out-pensioners, average expenditure per out-pensioner.

	Inmates						Out-pensioners					
	(1) Number	(2) Number	(3) Total Expenditure £	(4) Total Expenditure £	(5) Expenditure per £ s. d.	(6) Expenditure per £ s. d.	(7) Number	(8) Number	(9) Total Expenditure £	(10) Total Expenditure £	(11) Expenditure per £ s. d.	(12) Expenditure per £ s. d.
Year	Glasgow	Edinburgh	Glasgow	Edinburgh	Glasgow	Edinburgh	Glasgow	Edinburgh	Glasgow	Edinburgh	Glasgow	Edinburgh
1791	335	471	1903	3000	5 13 7	6 6 2	337		773	1186	2 6 0	
1792	363	464	1985	2788	5 9 5	6 0 2	341		730	809	2 2 10	
1793	375	493	2073	2858	5 10 7	5 16 0	352		825	400	2 6 10	
1794	384	484	2477	2359	6 9 8	4 17 5	563		1425	204	2 10 7	
1795	384	458	2463	2342	6 8 3	5 2 2	926		2266	236	2 8 10	
1796	377	422	2552	2812	6 15 4	6 13 2	903		2604	248	2 15 5	
1797	387	413	2644	2545	6 19 11	6 3 1	710		2101	287	2 19 0	
1798	396	417	2558	2747	6 9 3	6 11 10	699		1872	294	2 13 7	
1799	397	414	2667	2746	6 14 4	6 12 7	674		2024	309	3 0 0	
1800	395	420	3283	3349	8 6 3	7 19 5	728		3074	341	4 5 5	
1801	426	461	3879	4409	9 2 2	9 11 2	1050		5252	390	5 0 0	
1802	380	486	2803	3448	7 7 6	7 1 10	1128		3547	367	3 3 0	
1803	336		2517		7 9 10		711		1933		2 14 5	
1804	381		2890		7 11 9		784		2402		3 1 5	
1805	395		3179		8 0 11		800		2624		3 5 7	
1806	390		3070	3677	7 17 5		859		2492	505	2 18 0	
1807	394		3178	3665	8 1 4		651		2651	659	4 1 5	
1808	427	621	3494	3928	8 3 8	6 5 7	882	379	3181	900	3 12 2	2 7 5
1809	412	684	3430	5139	8 4 11	7 10 2	818	510	3363	1226	4 2 2	2 8 0
1810	420	724	3362	6465	8 0 0	8 18 7	932	616	3472	1461	3 14 6	2 7 5
1811	441	709	3476	5067	7 18 0	7 3 0	969	575	3546	1356	3 13 2	2 7 2
1812	470	741	4083	4841	8 13 9	6 10 7	1333	661	4878	1420	3 13 2	2 3 0
1813	482	842	4644		9 12 8		1329	708	6158		4 12 10	
1814	430	917	4260		9 18 2		1409	823	5494		3 17 10	
1815	436	856	4010		9 3 11		1208	896	4668		3 17 10	
1816	426	837	3904		9 3 3		1201	938	4048		3 5 5	
1817	497	884	4508		9 1 5		1079	997	6764		6 5 5	

SOURCES: Ewing, *Town's Hospital of Glasgow*, between pp. 178–79; ECW for each year.

depression in economic activity from 1815-18. Sharp decreases in this category of paupers can be accounted for by improvements in conditions and sharper scrutinies of the rolls. The observed fluctuations do not necessarily mean that all the new cases were either able-bodied individuals receiving temporary assistance or other individuals outwith the category of those legally entitled to relief. Most of the increase was probably due to proper recipients who under normal conditions were relieved by friends and relatives who were unable to offer the same assistance during periods of economic stress.

The minutes of the Edinburgh area workhouses provide information on the characteristics of inmates. The largest group of inmates consisted of women (over one-half of the total for Edinburgh and one-half to one-third for Canongate), then that consisting of boys and girls under 14 (approximately evenly divided between the two) and finally that of the men; only in Canongate did the total number of boys and girls exceed the number of women. The vast majority of inmates of the St. Cuthbert's Workhouse were either under the age of ten or over sixty. The fact that there were few children between ten and fourteen years of age indicates that children were apprenticed after reaching the age of ten. The following are the age and sex characteristics for the out-pensioners of the Edinburgh Charity Workhouse for 1840: 817 were female, 168 were male, their ages were nearly evenly distributed over the range from twenty-eight to eighty, but the bulk (or 437) of those under fifty received relief as either widows or widowers with a total of 992 dependent children. The average annual allowance for a single person with no dependents on the list was about £2 5s. 0d. The allowance for those with dependents varied according to the number and circumstances of the family.

Glasgow was spending more on its paupers than was Edinburgh, both in terms of total expenditure and expenditure per pauper. Comparing expenditure per inmate for Glasgow and Edinburgh [see Table II], the amounts for Glasgow generally exceed those for Edinburgh in spite of the fact that Edinburgh housed more inmates. The difference is very striking for 1808, when expenditure per inmate for Glasgow was £8 3s. 8d. and for Edinburgh was £6 5s 7d., the number of inmates being 427 and 621, respectively. Perhaps this can be attributed to the respective quality of conditions in the two institutions, implying that Glasgow made better provision for its inmates. Furthermore, the financial difficulties perpetually facing the directors of the Edinburgh Charity Workhouse suggest an inability to provide anything other than a minimum provision. Similar observations can be made about the expenditure per out-pensioner. It was cheaper to provide relief in the form of out-pensions, as the expenditure per out-pensioner was less than half that per inmate. The reason for this being, of course, that the whole maintenance of inmates had to be provided, whereas out-pensioners received assistance from other sources.

The question arises whether differences in relief payments between Edinburgh and Glasgow can be explained in terms of economic activity? Both cities were expanding during the period, though Glasgow's rate of growth was faster. These years could be called the "golden age" for Edinburgh, as the development of the New Town (construction started in 1769 and continued throughout the period), Leith Docks (1799-1817), and other substantial public work projects were undertaken, all of which absorbed workers during times of industrial unemployment. In Glasgow the tobacco trade was dying, but the cotton textile industry was beginning, resulting in tremendous industrial expansion. Remembering that the aged were the main recipients of relief and that their families were expected to provide all possible assistance, it is possible that the large scale public work projects of Edinburgh permitted lower relief payments by assuring steadier working-class incomes.

Factors which affected attitudes towards the poor, however, may

have been more important. Glasgow was a city with many businessmen
and merchants who had made large fortunes and were willing to risk
them in the hope of increasing them, as opposed to the conservative,
professional class make-up of Edinburgh. Glasgow did not have the
Edinburgh counterpart of the College of Justice, which steadfastly
refused to waive their right of exemption from the poor's tax. Nor
was Glasgow faced, as was Edinburgh, with a corrupt, debt-ridden
town council bent on creating financial difficulties for the
administrators of poor relief by refusing to impose the necessary
rates of assessment in order to secure adequate revenue for the
minimal operational requirements. Glasgow made provision for medical
relief for the out-pensioners by dividing the city into districts and
assigning surgeons to each; medical relief in Edinburgh was provided
on a voluntary basis by the surgeons. Thus, possibly Glasgow was
more charitable than Edinburgh.

Scotland's major burghs developed a system of workhouses,
starting in 1731. These institutions, however, over time evolved
into hospitals, as they were not feasible as productive units, given
the nature of the inmates. In all cases the workhouse inhabitants
were mainly the aged, the orphaned young, and the disabled. Out-
door relief became necessary as the burgh's populations increased
and the extent of pauperism exceeded the capacity of the workhouses.
Indoor relief remained, however, as a means test. Not surprisingly,
Glasgow placed a greater emphasis on the granting of out-door relief
than did Edinburgh; the problems of destitution should have been
greater in Glasgow because of the rapid population growth due to
industrialisation. Each burgh, therefore, developed a system of
poor relief suitable to its own needs.

---

1.   Minutes of the Directors of the Town's Hospital, MSS.,
     Mitchell Library, Glasgow, 6th November, 1818.

2. See Chapter 6.

3. St. Cuthbert's Charity Workhouse Minutes, 5th October, 1790,
    2nd January, 4th August and 6th October, 1801.

4. Select Committee on the Destitute Inhabitants of Paisley,
    Parliamentary Paper, 1843 (115), vol. VII, p. 7.

5. Select Committee, pp. 18-19. For a more detailed review of
    Paisley see Chapter 7 and T. C. Smout, ed., *The Search for
    Wealth and Stability*, London, 1979.

CHAPTER 4: THE ROLE OF PRIVATE CHARITIES

Private charity played an important role in augmenting the
statutory provision of poor relief. Indeed, the boundaries between the
two were often indistinct, making it difficult to judge the extent of
private charity, particularly with the scanty evidence available. Nonetheless, some indications of its significance and effectiveness can be
given. Most people argued that it was christian to be charitable.
Furthermore, private charity was regarded as the best form of charity,
as far as it could be extended, for "It cultivates, while it gratifies,
benevolence on the part of the giver, and induces gratitude on the
part of the receiver".[1] But an anonymous writer felt that in an age
of affluence the rich need diversions, hence they create private
charities: "Philanthropy is therefore the foible of the present
age".[2] He continued by stating,

> I fear this public mode of exercising charity will do
> much to diminish the extent of private benevolence.
> Benevolence exerted in secret is attended with no
> display; it may indeed purchase the blessing of the
> poor, but it brings no applause to its author. There
> is show and pomp however in a public contribution; and
> a man by subscribing his guinea, gets his name and his
> liberality published in the newspaper. He has likewise
> a chance of being elected to an office; and it gives
> one an air of superior wisdom, to be a manager or
> curator, to be a member of committees and councils.
> The vanity of this public charity deadens the
> conscience of many a man otherwise well disposed;
> it transforms a modest virtue into a gaudy vice; and
> makes a duty which ought to originate in tender pity,
> flow from the impure spring of ostentation.

Private charity can be defined, for our purposes, as all aid to
the poor, either monetary or non-monetary, supplied from sources other
than those specifically mentioned in the law as belonging to the
poor's fund. Furthermore, charity is a gift for which no return is
expected, and it can be bestowed either in an unorganised, individual
fashion or by a group organised for a stated purpose. The existence
of charities and the form they assume depend to a large extent upon
the development of the market economy. Unorganised charity

constitutes the bulk of private philanthropy. It includes not only
the occasional, indiscriminate hand-out to a beggar, but also any
non-reciprocal exchange among relatives and friends in times of need.
It plays a crucial role in man's well-being, for rarely are the old,
infirm, and orphaned left to fend for themselves in times of need.
Assistance in small communities was forthcoming without the necessity
to form consciously an "action group". It is not measurable because
of its whimsical nature.

Poor laws were the result of differing groups combining into a
nation, creating some form of surplus and recognising a need to ensure
a semblance of equity in caring for the weaker members. The passage
of such laws did not imply that private charity had ceased to function;
rather, they were an attempt to reinforce the attributes of private
charity. Charities served another purpose: to fulfil a need which
developed because of failures within the poor law to meet adequately
the needs of the poor. This is clearly seen in the operation of the
Scottish poor law, which placed a primary reliance on private charity.
Casual charity was able to cope efficiently with the situation only
as long as communities remained small and simple in structure.
Failure in large cities to meet the poor's needs is clear from the
case of Edinburgh where, in 1840, in only three out of 120 poor
families was there regular assistance from friends and relatives not
living in the family.[3] With the advent of industrialisation and
substantial and rapid urbanisation the need for a more formalised
means of private giving became apparent. To meet this need, new
charities were established on a more formal basis. Their primary
function was to ensure that the money collected for charitable
purposes was wisely spent. The individual donor no longer tried to
assess the need and moral character of the recipient: the
administrators of organised charities were supposed to be able to
judge the merits of each case.

Basically, organised charities can be divided into two groups, preventive and positive. Educational and religious charities are intended to be preventive in that they attempt to instil into individuals sound morals, and, more important, provide the tools for obtaining a livelihood. Positive charities are those which grant assistance in times of need, keeping the recipient from becoming a pauper. The funds for both groups generally were derived from public subscriptions, the donor in effect, purchasing the right to recommend individuals for assistance. Periodic sermons preached for specified charities were another popular form of raising revenue, illustrated by numerous advertisements in newspapers. Other sources of funds included church collections, charity balls, and concerts of sacred music.

Preventive charities particularly appealed to the Scots, for their purpose was to help the poor to help themselves. The first society in Scotland of this kind was concerned with supplying a religious education. One of the main functions of the Society in Scotland for Propogating Christian Knowledge, founded in 1709, was to supply parishes with schoolmasters and books. The need to establish such a charity was indeed a reflection that the provision for parochial education contained in the first book of discipline of John Knox had failed. The S.S.P.C.K.'s activities were not confined solely to Highland areas, for they made annual provision for educating the children in the Canongate Charity Workhouse.

The need to provide poor children with either a free education or one at a nominal charge was clearly recognised before 1800. Charity schools were established in numerous parishes, financed by voluntary subscriptions and extra-ordinary church collections. Similarly, numerous schools were founded and financed from mortified funds. Two examples are Wilson's Charity School for boys founded in 1778 and Millar's Charity School for girls founded in 1790, both in

Glasgow. The following extract indicates the conditions under which a boy could be enrolled in Wilson's School:

> No boys are to be admitted to this charity below six, or above seven, and perhaps the first year, eight years of age. Nor any who have the benefit either of Hutcheson's Hospital or of the Town's Hospital, or whose parents are not able to maintain them with food and lodging while they are at school.[4]

Both schools annually advertised vacant positions for students and gave the conditions for admission.

Another important form of charity intended to promote self-help was savings banks. These institutions can be classified as charities as they were designed to accept small deposits and guarantee their safety without the cost of transactions falling on depositors. The organisers appealed to the wealthier classes for both funds and voluntary help to run the system. They were designed to help the lower classes to save during their more prosperous periods with the hope of preventing them from becoming paupers in bad times, or in old age. Indeed it was suggested that there was a correlation between an increase in deposits and a diminution in the poor rates.[5] The importance of savings banks and their effect upon the poor rates was the subject of a parliamentary debate in 1817. Wilberforce argued that a system of banks would contribute to the abolition of the rates, and that a feeling of independence would be nurtured. Sir Charles Monck countered that it was an idle dream to think that the rates would be eliminated by savings banks.[6] Sir Gerard Noel writing to the *Scotsman* felt that such banks would be used against the poor unable to save, for when forced to enter a workhouse they would be soundly rebuked for a failure to provide for their old age. Furthermore, savings banks should not be initiated during a period of need. "The people have little to thank their rich neighbours for in this anxiety for the poor *to take care of themselves*, and to deposit their little hoards in the hands of those who are the authors of their

poverty."[7]   Rev. Henry Duncan first introduced savings banks in
Scotland when he opened one in the parish of Ruthwell, Dumfrieshire
in 1810. By 1818 there were over 130 savings banks outside of Glasgow
and Edinburgh. It should be noted that the first site of the Aberdeen
Savings Bank was located in the City's poor house, a factor probably
causing a negative effect upon the propensity of the "respectable"
poor to use the Bank.

Preventive charities are generally of a self-help nature, but
positive charities usually are not, since the recipient has reached
a state of severe destitution. Not all positive charities, however,
meet this description: friendly societies were established for the
purpose of relieving members during periods of distress. In exchange
for this service the member paid an initiation fee and annual dues,
thus purchasing insurance against loss of income from sickness or
other causes. In Glasgow the first friendly society, Bell's Wynd
Society, was formed in 1746; by 1828 the number had increased to
129. Clearly, they played an important role in providing assistance.

The fourteen Incorporated Trades in Glasgow had procedures for
caring for their destitute members. A member applied for relief by
petition to the deacon or master of his trade, who appointed a
committee to investigate the case. If relief was granted, the
recipient was enrolled on a weekly, monthly, or quarterly list,
the amount varying among the trades, from 5s. per quarter to 6s. per
week. In 1819 the Trades distributed £2848 11s. 3d. to 876 persons.
In addition to this amount the Incorporation of Tailors gave their
usual annual distribution of fifty pounds to the poor on their rolls.
Members of the Merchants' House had to pay a poor rate to the House
of 5s. entry money and 4s. yearly thereafter. Failure to pay
resulted in a loss of voting rights.

Hospitals developed as a means of caring for the sick poor, many
assuming the characteristics of legal public relief, except that the

funds were drawn from voluntary subscriptions and the administration
was independent of the poor law. One of the earliest hospitals in
Scotland was Trinity in Edinburgh, established about 1460 for the
purpose of housing the sick, pilgrims, orphaned children, aged and
infirm poor. In 1579 the Edinburgh town council became the
administrators. They decided that the Hospital would not maintain
out-pensioners and that only burgesses would be admitted, provided
all their goods became the property of the Hospital. The revenue was
derived from the rental of mortified lands and donations. Although
the inmates were considered to be a class superior to those in the
Edinburgh Charity Workhouse, Arnot, writing in 1780, stated that
their behaviour was deplorable and they were only a 'cut above the
vulgar'.[8]

The Glasgow Lunatic Asylum was rather curiously organised: it
was constructed mainly for the rich, but provision was made for
pauper lunatics, their maintenance cost defrayed from the public
legal funds, though the administration was separate. Parishes
outwith Glasgow could have their pauper lunatics admitted at the
same rates by making a fifty pound contribution. In 1815 the number
of paupers lodged in the Asylum was so great that several were in
rooms furnished for patients of higher ranks; if any person of the
latter category were to apply for admission, the paupers would have
to be dismissed and admitted only in order of application.

The Edinburgh Public Dispensary, open four days a week in order
to give free advice, was established in 1776 by Dr Duncan for the
poor whose diseases were such as to render their admission into the
Royal Infirmary either unnecessary or improper. The expenses were
met by public contributions and small fees from students who attended
lectures. It was managed by a president, two vice-presidents, and
twenty directors elected annually from among the contributors. One
guinea entitled a contributor to recommend patients and to be a

governor for two years; a contribution of five guineas gave the same
privileges for life.

The Paisley Female Benevolent Society was founded in November 1811
for the purpose of providing assistance to aged indigent females in the
Paisley area. Their funds were derived from public subscriptions and
between 1811 and 1818 amounted to an average of three hundred pounds
per year. In 1818, 534 females were relieved, principally with clothes,
coal and other provisions. Monthly visitors inquired into the
recipients' circumstances, those of bad character being denied relief.
The visitors tried to persuade the applicant's friends and relatives
to provide some assistance. In fact the duties of the visitors were
considered so demanding that people were found only after great
difficulty. Finally, the Society was concerned with the moral welfare
of its recipients; all were supplied with Bibles.

Unemployed labourers presented a special problem, as they were
not eligible for relief from the legal funds. Therefore, during
periods of large scale unemployment, committees were established to
raise funds by voluntary subscription and distribute them to the
unemployed. An example is the Edinburgh Committee for Relief of
Labouring Classes, founded in 1816. Between 16th December, 1816 and
17th March, 1817 subscriptions totalling £7188 1s. 6d. were received,
of which £6813 14s. 0d. was expended on 1798 persons. The Committee
employed 1100 in outdoor work and paid them 5-6s. per week, besides
giving those with families an allowance of soup, meal, and coal
proportional to the number in the family. The epidemic in Glasgow
in 1832 was responsible for a number of soup kitchens being established
to aid labourers finding it inconvenient to cook in small quantities.
The "Barley Broth Kitchen" on Great Clyde Street daily distributed
bread and 600 quarts of broth. A kitchen managed by a Mr Menzies
also distributed soap, informing the recipient that dirty individuals
would not receive soup. All the kitchens gave weekly tickets, those

not wishing free soup could buy tickets.

Hundreds of charities existed all over Scotland; their common feature was the similarity in the managerial structure with that of the legal funds. This, combined with a system of inter-locking directorates, enabled poor rates to be kept to a minimum by referring applicants for public relief to an appropriate charity. Captain Thomson, treasurer of the Edinburgh House of Refuge, stated that at least one-third of the persons who applied for admission were eligible for public assistance.[9]

James Cleland made several attempts to measure the extent of private charity in Glasgow. His calculations for 1815-16 for organised charities, where the expenditure was known, give the total expenditure as being £19,654 12s. 4d. Comparing this amount with total public relief expenditure of £13,388 19s. 8d., one can see that the amount supplied by organised charities was nearly one and a half times that of public relief. He estimated that supplies forthcoming from unorganised sources totalled £67,667 12s. 0d.[10] Cleland's calculations were probably realistic when one remembers that families often gave old clothes to relatives, friends, or servants, besides assistance during sickness.

An idea of the number of persons relieved is obtained from Alison, who gave the following table for a few of Edinburgh's charitable associations in 1831:[11]

Destitute Sick Society	10,500
Strangers' Friend Society	1,900
House of Refuge	1,200
Night Refuge	600
Royal Infirmary	2,000
Society for Incurables	100
Female and Old Man's Societies	200
Society for Clothing Industrious Poor	200
Subscriptions raised last winter for relieving the most destitute of the poor	5,000
Total relieved not less than	21,700

In the same year the number relieved by the legal funds in the Edinburgh area was 5,004. These figures provide an idea of the extent of destitution, and indicate the degree to which the legal funds were inadequate, besides the vital role played by private charity in providing assistance to the poor of Scotland. Without it many of them would not have been able to survive. Indeed, the existence of these charities enabled the administrators of the legal public funds to maintain their minimal allowances long after industrialisation and a changing price structure had made them totally inadequate even by the standards of the day.

1. Robert Hamilton, *An Address to the Inhabitants of Aberdeen on the Management of the Poor*, p. 20.

2. Anon [Dr Crawford], *The Attic Stories, or the opinions of Edward Hazelrig, Esq.*, pp. 198-9.

3. W.P. Alison, "Illustrations of the Practical Operation of the Scottish System of Management of the Poor", in *Quarterly Journal of the Statistical Society of London*, vol. 3, 1840. p. 225.

4. *Glasgow Mercury*, 8th June, 1780.

5. Albert Fishlow, "The Trustee Savings Bank, 1817-1861", in *JEH*, 1961, p. 26.

6. *Scotsman*, 16th February, 1817.

7. Sir Gerard Noel, "Savings Banks and other Ministerial Expedients and Delusions", in *Scotsman*, 28th March, 1818.

8. James Colston, *Trinity College and Trinity Hospital*, vol. 1, p. 22.

9. *Report of the Association for obtaining Inquiry into Pauperism in Scotland*, p. 5.

10. James Cleland, *Annals of Glasgow*, pp. 270-4.

11. W.P. Alison, "Illustrations", p. 248.

Much has been written about the English poor law; indeed so much emphasis has been laid upon it in historical discussion in both Britain and North America that the erroneous impression may have been gained by some that the system was applied to all parts of the United Kingdom. An outline of the major English poor relief legislation, followed by a comparison with the Scottish experience, reveals differences between the two systems that are striking and important.

A. *The English Poor Law Prior to 1834*

The first English statute to be considered is 14 Elizabeth, c. 5 [1572]. This Act, entitled "An Act for the Punishment of Vagabonds, and for Relief of the Poor and Impotent", is important in that its wording is reproduced in a nearly identical manner in the Scottish Acts of 1574 and 1579. This English Act may well be in part derivative, being remarkably like that of Emperor Charles V. of Holland, brought into effect on 7th October, 1531.

In this Act of Elizabeth, as with previous English Acts, begging was a licensed activity. Every person above fourteen years of age found begging without a license was to be committed to jail till the next session, and if convicted, he was for the first offence to be whipped and burnt through the gristle of the right ear with a hot iron one inch in compass, unless some person of honest repute was to take him into continuous service for one year. For the second offence he was to be judged a felon and suffer as such, unless taken into service for two years. For the third offence he was to suffer death and loss of land and goods, without benefit of clergy or sanctuary. Those defined as rogues, vagabonds and sturdy beggars included idle persons going about using "subtle craft" and "unlawful games", all persons able in body but having neither land nor master, nor able to give an account of how they earned their living, and all common labourers loitering and refusing to work for the wages commonly given. Conviction of harbouring or relieving such individuals brought a penalty of 20s. Sterling.

After declared hostility to the sturdy beggars, the Act turned to aged and impotent poor persons. All such should be supplied with provisions and a convenient abiding place, so that none should have to beg or wander about. The justices of the peace were to compile a register of those impotent poor persons who had lived in their district for the last three years and from this list to determine the weekly amount necessary for their relief and sustenance. The justices were also empowered to tax the inhabitants within the division for the necessary amount, to appoint tax collectors, and to make a required annual appointment of overseers of the poor. It was further ordained that those poor who were able to do some work would be required to earn part of their livelihood; if they refused to work, they were to be whipped and stocked for the first refusal and to be treated as vagabonds for the second.

The Tudors placed primary emphasis upon discouraging vagabondage by severely punishing all rogues, vagabonds and sturdy beggars, but it eventually became apparent that in the presence of actual want, punishment was not a deterrent for begging and vagabondage. In the light of this realisation and largely as a measure for protecting the security of the monarchy, the conviction developed that the first step in curbing the undesirable activities of begging and vagabondage was to ensure that no extremity of want should arise. Therefore measures were taken which would leave no alternative between starvation and a breach of the law. These ideas are reflected in the codifying statute of 43 Elizabeth, c. 2, [1601], which sets forth the principle that the relief of destitution must be undertaken as a public duty and be provided for at the public expense.

The Act of 1601 established the parish as the unit of

administration and declared that each parish was to provide work for
the able-bodied unemployed, to provide for the old and infirm, and to
provide technical education for poor children in the form of
apprenticeships. Under the Act the parish magistrates were to appoint
each year two or more inhabitants as overseers for the poor, an office
lacking monetary compensation.

The overseers had the right to levy upon the inhabitants of the
parish a tax in order to meet the relief expenditure. They, along
with the magistrates, had absolute power over the poor and in assessing the poor rates. The overseers, within four days after the end of
a year of service, were to present to two magistrates a full accounting of poor funds received and expended. If a parish was unable to
gather sufficient funds, the magistrates were empowered to tax
neighbouring parishes within the hundred, and if that was insufficient,
the county was taxed. This "Rate in Aid" clause, however, seldom
was used. The magistrates could issue a warrant of distress for
recovering the non-payment of taxed sums and could commit to prison
the offender until the assessed amount was paid. They could also
imprison any able-bodied poor person who refused work ordered by the
overseers. The parish now had a responsibility for the able-bodied
unemployed.

Since it was argued that children should be put to work as soon
as possible, because their being educated was a waste to society and
the failure to put them to work would encourage idleness, the Act
provided for the apprenticing of children of seven years or more. The
overseers, with the consent of two justices, were empowered to bind
into apprenticeship all children whose parents could not maintain
them. Males were apprenticed until the age of twenty-four and females
until the age of twenty-one or marriage.

The impact of the 1601 Act should not be measured by its
immediate effects. Although the principles of the Act were

revolutionary, especially the section providing employment for the able-bodied unemployed, its importance lies in the fact that its philosophy dominated English poor law legislation for some three hundred years. The Act, however, appears to have failed in solving the problem of rogues and vagabonds.

Little happened in the way of poor law legislation during the Interregnum. The next major provision was "An Act for the Better Relief of the Poor", 14 Charles II., c. 12 [1662], the important statute by which settlement and the power of removal were first legally established: it has been popularly named 'The Settlement Act'. Although it deals with several facets of poor relief, its most important aspect concerns the authority given to overseers over any person who had settled in a tenement with a yearly value under ten pounds, and who was likely to become chargeable to the parish: the overseers, with the consent of two justices, could, within forty days, remove any such person to his place of original settlement. The only exception was that during harvest time a person could travel to another parish to work, provided he carried a certificate attesting to his parish of settlement.

George Coode, Esq., in his *Report to the Poor Law Board on the law of Settlement* in 1851, described the origin and results of the Settlement Act. He felt that the Act was a result of action by the metropolitan members of Parliament who wanted to relieve the increasing pressure of poor persons in London and Westminster, by enabling the poor to be removed to the country parishes where they were legally settled. Thus, the Act was seen as a logical culmination of measures to prevent the convergence on London of the unemployed. The harvest-time exception was believed to have been a compromise measure to secure the support of country members.

Prior to the 1662 Act the poor could seek employment anywhere, and only individuals unwilling to work were forced to live in their parish of settlement. After 1662 however, any poor persons who migrated from their parish of settlement were liable for removal back to that parish. Furthermore, since the parish of settlement was charged for the removal expenses incurred, the probability of removal was high. In 1691 the law was changed so that the forty day period, during which persons likely to become chargeable to the parish must be removed, was defined as beginning with a public reading by the individual of his intent to settle. An Act in 1695 made it possible for people to migrate to another parish if their parish of settlement issued a certificate to their parish of residence. (As noted below, 'parish of settlement' was a legal term, therefore it was possible for a person's parish of residence to be different from his parish of settlement.) But the first major change in the settlement laws was not until 1795, when it was declared that a person could not legally be removed until he actually became chargeable, and that the parish of settlement did not have to pay the removal expenses incurred. Settlement laws remained in effect in some form until as late as 1876.

Normally an individual's parish of settlement was determined either by his place of birth, or, in the case of a married woman, by her husband's parish, or by residing in a parish for forty days after reading a statement of intent to settle. The 1691 Act provided the following four additional means of gaining settlement in another parish: (1) by being taxed at parish rates and paying those rates, (2) by being elected to an annual parish office and serving in that office for a year, (3) by serving an apprenticeship in the parish, and (4) by working in a job continuously for at least a year. The place of settlement for a bastard was his mother's parish, otherwise children were settled in their father's parish. Occasionally there arose problems of settlement not without comedy. For example if an individual rented a tenement worth ten pounds which was situated in two parishes, his parish of settlement was the parish in which his bed was located. Thus to change his parish of settlement, it was only

necessary to move his bed to the other parish.[1]

Enforcing the settlement laws was both expensive and time

consuming, as can be seen from the following quotation:

> From 1776 to 1815 the annual expense of litigation grew
> from £35,000 to £287,000. Constables in parishes on
> main roads sometimes spent the whole of their time
> transporting paupers, counties and parishes entered into
> pauper removal contracts with business men who special-
> ised in the work.... Half the business of every quarter
> sessions consisted in deciding appeals on orders of
> removal, at an expense which, so it was alleged, would
> in many cases have covered the entire cost of the
> pauper's maintenance several times over and still left
> the contesting parishes a handsome profit.[2]

For approximately one hundred years after the 1662 Act there was

a striking lack of innovation. Such Acts as were passed during this

period consisted primarily of re-wording previous statutes. An Act in

1722 gave parishes permission to join together and build workhouses,

and gave the overseers permission to deny relief to all who refused

to enter them. This was later reversed.

In 1795 the magistrates of the parish of Speenhamland in the

county of Berkshire, in an attempt to improve the conditions of

agricultural labourers due to low wages and high prices caused by the

Napoleonic wars and bad harvests, adopted a system of out-door relief

designed to furnish a minimum standard of living. Thus, primarily

for humanitarian reasons, the magistrates decided to provide relief

in the form of wage supplements and published their table of rates.

The idea was to guarantee a subsistence level of income by augmenting

wages when earnings fell below the established subsistence level. The

level of aid was determined by the price of bread and the number of

dependents of the head of the household. For the next several years

the use of allowances-in-aid-of-wages tied to a proxy for a cost-of-

living index gained greater use until, if we are to believe the results

of the questionnaire sent to parishes by the 1824 Committee on

Labourers' Wages, the Speenhamland System was extensively practised in eighteen English counties.

Although wage supplements were not new (several parishes adopted them after the 1871 Act gave authority to do so), Speenhamland was the first instance of established, published rates based upon a bread scale. This action was probably responsible for the spread of the use of wage supplements. Thus, there was a break from the old form of relief through providing work for the unemployed (either requiring farmers to hire unemployed workers or providing work otherwise through the parish) and giving relief under supervision in workhouses. The bread scale never received statutory authority. Other parishes either adopted the Speenhamland scale, devised their own scale, or based wage supplements on some other standard. Relief was in the form of either money or flour. In some parishes it was given for children only after a certain number in the family was exceeded. But the characteristic which all Speenhamland counties held in common was the practice of giving relief in the form of wage supplements.

The funds for relief payments were obtained by taxing the occupiers of the land in each parish. Since the laws were vague as to what the rates were to be based on, the principle of assessment varied from parish to parish. The means used included levying the assessed rates on annual rent paid, land tax, stock in trade, personal property, and real property. It appears that the most popular approach was to assess the value of real property. Some parishes besides assessing a rate tax, also grew crops, of which a portion was given to the poor and the remainder sold. The occupiers of land in some parishes had an alternative to paying the poor rate tax: they could hire a certain number of unemployed workers at a set wage.

It is important to note that a vigourous attack upon the Speenhamland System did not begin until after the Napoleonic wars had ended. But from 1815 there was a growing concern over the high and increasing relief expenditure. Commissions in 1818 and 1824

criticized the use of allowances-in-aid-of-wages and expressed a need
to adopt the parochial system of Scotland. The final blow came in
1832, when the Poor Law Commission began collecting in their view
"insurmountable" evidence that the System was demoralising workers,
inducing population growth, lowering wages, and, in short, was so bad
that it should be abolished. As a result, in 1834 the Poor Law
Amendment Act was passed.

This Act abolished the parish as the principal unit of
administration and established unions of parishes. A commission of
three members was appointed to direct poor law policy at the national
level. The Commission ordered that all out-door relief, and especially
allowance systems, be abandoned; workhouses were to be established,
and all relief was to be given in them. It had been argued that
workhouses never became a reality on a large scale, for parishes found
that it was cheaper to provide out-door relief in the form of wage
supplements, than to provide workhouses where one-hundred per cent
of the poor's expenses had to be met.[3] Thus, the results which the
drafters of the 1834 Act hoped to achieve were not obtained.

B. *A Comparison of the Two Systems*

Until 1834 the administration of relief in rural areas in both
Scotland and England was at the parish level. The English overseers
were appointed to office on an annual basis by the justices of the
peace, and on these overseers depended the operation of the law.
They were legally compelled to serve, unpaid, for only a year, though
they could be excused if they paid a fine. By this means the men
most capable of serving escaped the unpleasant, time consuming
business. Thus, most overseers were unfamiliar with the operation of
public administration, being farmers engaged in earning their own
living, and unwilling to devote much time to the troublesome duties
of overseer. Moreover, as the duration of the office was for only

one year, most overseers were unwilling to experiment, wishing to end their year of service with as little difficulty as possible. Economy was not forced upon them as the funds they administered were limited only by public opinion and the ability of ratepayers to pay. As the paupers could appeal to the justices of the peace concerning the amount of their allowance, the overseers were often willing to grant liberal payments in order to prevent being summoned before the justice.

By contrast the Scottish elders were the respected men of the parish and were appointed for life, enabling them to become familiar with the needs of the inhabitants and providing an element of continuity in the administration. They were left with a free hand in administering relief, unless there was a threat of a legal assessment, at which time the heritors assumed an active role in the parochial affairs. The heritors provided a check on expenditure as they paid one-half of any stent levied for poor relief. Hence they had a direct interest in keeping relief payments at a low level. Thus in Scotland relief was administered by the co-operation of the most influential men of the parish. Any person who felt that he had not received a fair hearing by the kirk session and heritors, could appeal directly to the Court of Session, without having to incur any expenses.

The English never relied on voluntary contributions as a source of funds; they employed a compulsory assessment, levied on the inhabitants of the parish by the overseers. Because an overseer might not be a ratepayer, and because he held office for only a year, he felt little compulsion to keep the rates and levels of expenditure low.

In Scotland the prime method of financing poor relief expenditure was a reliance on voluntary contributions. The Scots felt that the strength of their system lay in the voluntary nature of the funds;

there were dangers in relying on a compulsory assessment. With
voluntary contributions the poor would be grateful for assistance;
with an assessment it was feared they would demand relief as a right.
Hence, a legal assessment would debase the morals of the lower classes,
causing them to demand relief, thereby drastically increasing relief
expenditure.

Both countries recognised the right of the aged, young orphans,
the impotent, the crippled, and the blind to receive relief. But in
terms of legislation the English took the crucial further step of
requiring that aid be given to the able-bodied unemployed. The
Scottish denial to this category of relief was adhered to in the
legislation, but not in practice. The first mention of relief to the
able-bodied unemployed in the English statutes was in the 1601 Act,
which ordained that the parish was to provide work for the unemployed.
Even though later legislation stated that relief was to be provided
in workhouses, out-door relief was the most common means of providing
employment. With the 1781 Act parishes were permitted to augment the
wages of the lowest paid workers; this established the principle that
the able-bodied were entitled to relief in spite of being employed and
reportedly led to an increase in the amounts of relief given, resulting
eventually in the change in the law in 1834.

In terms of expenditure levels the English were spending more on
relief per head of population before 1815 than were the Scots. But,
there was a startling convergence of the amounts after 1815. The
decrease in the English figures can be explained by the effective
debates on the Speenhamland System in 1818. Perhaps, also, the
English were paying heed to the arguments that the Scottish system
was preferable, hence aiming at its expenditure levels. This latter
point is supported by the admiration for the Scottish system as
expressed in the Select Committee Report of 1817; the impact of this
Report is discussed in Chapter 7.

It is clear from the numerous Acts passed in the 15th and 16th centuries that the Scots, like the English, were plagued, or at least felt they were plagued with a serious and apparently insoluble problem of vagabonds and strong beggars. These Acts provided various types of severe corporal and capital punishment as a means of deterring begging, numerous re-enactments suggesting a failure in the achievement of their purposes. In these Acts, as in all later poor law legislation, the Scots made a distinction between those able to earn their own livelihood and those unable to support themselves by useful work. The laws stated that only those between the ages of fourteen and seventy, who could not earn their subsistence by any other means, were allowed to beg, thus creating the embryo of a system of poor relief, albeit only by the means of legalised begging.

The basis of the Scottish poor law was the Act of 1574, its wording nearly identical to that of 14 Elizabeth, c. 5 [1572]. This similarity is not surprising in the light of the political situation at the time. Mary had been deposed as Queen because of her pro-Catholic leanings, and as James was still an infant, Scotland was ruled by regents. The Earl of Mar was Regent in 1574, the Earl of Morton in 1579. Both men, especially Morton, were protestants and looked to Elizabeth for support. Morton desired to see James succeed Elizabeth, hence it was only natural for Scottish Acts passed during this period to reflect English philosophy.

Initially, the administration of the Scottish law was left to the justices of the peace in the rural parishes and the magistrates and town councils in the burghs. In legislation for the burghs the administrators were never changed, but in the rural parishes the Act of 1594 changed the administration to the individual kirk sessions. Although by this time Presbyterianism was firmly established in Scotland, this was a curious move, as James VI was currently engaged in struggles which were to diminish the powers of the General

Assembly of the Church of Scotland. The heritors were not made joint administrators with the kirk sessions until the Act of 1672, implying that the heritors were included because of increasing pressures to impose a legal assessment, and hence a feeling that the largest group of taxpayers should be represented to ensure a careful watch on expenditure.

Scottish legislation was similar to the English during periods of episcopalian ascendancy and was different during periods of presbyterian ascendency. The divergence of the two systems after 1603 also can be explained in part by the Anglicised monarchs caring little about Scotland. Any attempts to force their will upon the Scottish Parliament would have required their presence in Scotland, a prospect not particularly appealing to those enjoying the relative comforts of England. After the Union of Parliaments in 1707 the complete lack of legislation in Westminster concerning Scottish poor relief until 1845, in spite of prodigious amounts of English legislation, would be a further indication of the British monarchs' apparent lack of interest in the Scottish scene. Furthermore, most Englishmen during the eighteenth century were probably ignorant about and not interested in Scots law. This explains the initial movements in legislation and the lack of imposed legislation, but it fails to explain the lack of initiative on the part of the Scots.

Scotland's approach to the problems of poverty perhaps differed from the English because of differences of scale and stages of development. The smaller and less advanced the society, the less formal need be the system of poor relief. The English system reflected the imperatives of a larger society and one more advanced in specialisation through commerce and industry. Little wonder that opposition against the system as followed in Scotland gained numbers and strength only after the pressures of rapid urbanisation in the post-1800 period.

In terms of relief to the impotent the Scottish system was one of parochial paternalism where the elders were familiar with the conditions and needs of the inhabitants of the parish. This ideal situation was possible as long as the population of the parish was relatively small. But the parochial system could not cope with densely populated urban areas which forced the creation of a system where paid overseers implemented the policy decisions of voluntary managers. In other words increased population brought a greater formalisation of the law.

The population of the parishes in England had long reached the critical level, and this was reflected by the passing of numerous Acts designed to formalise the system and enable it to be uniformally administered by overseers, who were obliged to provide relief to the able-bodied during periods of sickness or unemployment. The market economy was at a stage of development where it was essential to maintain a large pool of both agricultural and industrial workers; the cities were large and dependent upon the rural areas for food supplies; unemployed workers required monetary assistance in the form of public relief. The 1834 English Act was an attempt to adopt the individualism of the Scottish system. The failure to implement the Act's provisions reflects a need for formal public intervention within a complex social system. Scotland, too, had eventually to accept a far-reaching public responsibility.

What did the two systems learn from each other? If one were to examine just the legislation, it would seem that the answer would be not much, for in spite of a similar basic structure the legislation exhibits striking differences, with the English laws being more progressive and liberal. But in terms of practice little variation existed between the two, especially as the process of industrialisation intensified. Both systems recognised the need to provide relief to the able-bodied unemployed. Yet, there were elements in both countries which refused to recognise the occurrence of large-scale social and economic change. The English Select Committees in their Reports describe more the state of the Scottish legislation than actual practice. The 1834 English Act reflects an attempt to return to a previous *status quo*. As will be seen in the next several Chapters, the Scots also wished to turn back the clock by proposing legislation designed to preserve the essence of their envied parochial system and to prevent the proliferation of English practices. But the English Act of 1834 also was an attempt to achieve a degree of unification in poor law practice among the 15,000 English parishes. This was the purpose of the Board of Supervision. Less diversity in practice existed among the Scottish parishes, as there were only 850 parishes. The English did learn from the Scots that nearly equal treatment of the poor throughout the country was preferable to extreme diversity.

---

1. W. E. Tate, *The Parish Chest*, p. 200.

2. W. E. Tate, *The Parish Chest*, p. 200.

3. Michael Rose, "The Allowance System", in *EcHR* 1966, pp. 607-20.

An examination of pauperism in Scotland must include a discussion of the social philosophy of the country's famous divine, Thomas Chalmers [1780-1847], the most important personality in the realm of Scottish poor relief, whose following consisted of a large group of dedicated men. He represented and refined the old school of parochial relief, attempting to retain the principles of voluntary contributions and refusing to recognise the trends of industrial development.

Chalmers' numerous writings on poverty have been largely neglected by scholars; the last major work incorporating and upholding Chalmers' belief in a parochial system of relief was published over seventy years ago, during the debates which eventually culminated in the Poor Law of 1909, though all writers expounding the parochial system referred to the success of his famous Glasgow experiment, begun in 1819. But before attempting a revaluation of the St. John's experiment, it is necessary to present Chalmers' theories concerning pauperism.

Chalmers always made a distinction between poverty and pauperism. He wrote, "we are able to affirm, on the highest of all authorities, that the poor shall be with us always - or, in other words, that it is vain to look for the extinction of poverty from the world".[1] Yet, all his writings on this question were concerned with the establishment of a system which would eliminate pauperism. This apparent inconsistency is easily resolved, for Chalmers established that "a poor man is a man in want of adequate means for his own subsistence. A pauper is a man who has this want supplemented in whole or in part, out of a *legal* and *compulsory provision*" [italics added].[2] Hence, to be poor is primarily to be in want. This, of course, is a relative concept: any person who is unable to maintain himself in the average style of his class of society may be poor, for he wants what he lacks. If his needs were supplied by means other than funds obtained by an

authoritarian assessment, he would not be considered a pauper.
Therefore, pauperism implied the reception of public relief from funds
obtained by a legal assessment.

Given a state of poverty, Chalmers saw two 'springs' from which
charity might flow, the 'natural' and the 'artificial'. The former
eliminates the need, without producing pauperism, whereas the latter
creates a pauper. He argued that the development of an artificial
source of assistance through legal assessments caused the natural
source to 'dry up'. Thus, he advocated the abolition of such
assessments, thereby allowing the replenishment of the natural sources.
These sources were referred to as 'the four fountains'. They were
(1) the habits and economies of the people, (2) the kindness of
relatives, (3) the sympathy of the wealthy for the poorer classes,
and (4) the sympathy of the poor for one another. Pauperism reduces
or destroys their flow.

Chalmers gave four reasons why a system of relief based upon
compulsory assessments was doomed to failure: first, people become
systematically trained to expect relief as a right, therefore
destroying the connection which Nature has established between
economy and independence and between improvidence and want; second,
the neighbours and kindred of the poor lose their private sympathies
and abstain from providing relief; third, as the number of poor
increase, they will be less adequately relieved, as the allowance
per pauper tends to decrease; finally, an artificial system tends to
be wasteful, owing to the increase both in expenditure on paupers
demanding relief as a legal right, and in the number of individuals
needed to administer relief.

Another crucial factor was that the area of administration should
be small, since, by having such units, "Pauperism would become less
noxious, simply by throwing it into such a form as might make it less
noticeable".[3] Smaller units place the administrators in closer

contact with the people's needs, and the role of watchdog can be performed more efficiently.

According to the Bible, blessed are those who give. An individual must give generously. But he must be secret in his alms-giving. This represents the true spirit of philanthropy. But Chalmers had other reasons for advocating giving in secret: the public giver is assaulted with applications from false seekers, whereas the secret giver can quietly seek the 'true' deservers of relief.

But the recipient also has a responsibility. He should be humble and grateful for the assistance, no matter how insignificant in amount, and under no circumstances should he demand assistance as a right. Chalmers argued that public assistance caused persons to demand relief, even when they were not eligible for it, resulting in a loss of gratitude and respect for the giver. This was clearly an undesirable situation.

For Chalmers the achievement of a better system depended not merely on changing the mode of administration, but on changing the character of the fund. It should be freed from the attributes of certainty, legality, and apparent capability of infinite augmentation. Poor relief should stem from a voluntary fund, not from a legal assessment. And he believed that every extension of the poor's fund is followed by a more than proportional increase of actual poverty.

But the return to a voluntary system was only one fork in his two pronged attack on the elimination of pauperism. Education too played a crucial role in Chalmers' scheme. The most important aspect of education was to provide the pupils with a knowledge of the Bible. By using it as the major text, moral values would be instilled into the pupils. The teaching of reading, writing, and arithmetic played a secondary role. A good system should attempt to prevent pauperism, rather than relieve it, and the best method of prevention would be to encourage moral fortitude. "...the great instrument for thus elevating the poor, is that Gospel of Jesus Christ, which may be preached unto the poor."[4] He argued that schools should be endowed to the point where teachers were able to provide education for the people. This would be accomplished by continuing to provide enough buildings to meet the demand for education. The cost of the education should be paid for by small fees.

Chalmers' ideas were formed primarily between 1802 and 1815, while he was minister of the small, rural parish of Kilmany, Fife, though he did not begin to publish his views extensively until the 1820s. A study of his many volumes reveals the complete inflexibility of his social theories. He never publicly veered from his chosen position. The striking contrast between the administration of relief in Kilmany and that in Glasgow, where he moved in 1815, served to confirm his beliefs. After the simple, parsimonious system of Kilmany, Glasgow appeared as a nightmare, from which he quickly divorced himself. He informed the parishioners of the Tron that his duties were to look after their moral interest; the elders were to serve the poor.

At the time of his arrival in Glasgow poor relief was administered independently by the General Session and the Town's Hospital.[5] Chalmers reacted against this system because "...the more wide the field of superintendence is, the greater must be the moral distance between the administrators of the charity and its recipients".[6] Furthermore,

> ...each Session might have been regarded as having two
> doors - one of them a door of admittance from the
> population who stand at the margin of pauperism; and
> another of them, a door of egress to the Town Hospital,
> through which the occupiers of the outer court made
> their way to the inner temple.[7]

The individual sessions had no incentive to minimise the number on their roll, as there was no correlation between their collections and their number of paupers, and because the Hospital was regarded as a vast reservoir upon which they could draw. Chalmers felt that if each session was allowed to keep its collection, it would exhibit a greater interest in the management of relief. For these reasons he asked the magistrates and town council for permission to establish a new parish, St. John's, and to administer relief to the parish's paupers, independently of the current establishment, according to the principles of the parochial system, the rural method of relief he had known at Kilmany.

To implement his system, Chalmers partitioned St. John's into twenty-five districts and appointed a deacon to each as its overseer. (The office of deacon, fallen into disuse and now revived by Chalmers, was created by the First Book of Discipline of the Church for the purpose of serving the poor.) A detailed description of the parish is obtained from an 1819 survey.[8] It contained the following information for each of the twenty-five proportions: name and occupation, total number in house, number of sittings in church, place of worship, number of persons between six and fifteen, children above six unable to read and not at school, children attending Sabbath schools, and children not attending Sabbath schools. The survey was taken after the formation of the parish, but before the Church was opened for worship.

As the total population for the parish was 10,513 and there were 2,237 households, the average number of persons per house was 4.70. The tenth proportion had the greatest density of population with 5.91 persons per house and, indeed, the largest absolute population with 680 persons. The eighteenth proportion was the least dense with 3.59 persons per house. The population of the proportions varied from a low of 207 to a high of 680 and an average of 420.5. The details are contained in Table III.

TABLE III: Summary of Population Characteristics, by Proportion, St. John's Parish, Glasgow, 1819

Proportion	Population	Number of Households	Average number per house	Church Seats Church of Scotland	Church Seats Church of All other Churches	No. Seats	Percent. of Population without seats	Ratio Church seats (All Churches) (Church of Scotland)
1	339	77	4.40	33	88	201	59.3	2.67
2	335	75	4.47	47	104	189	56.4	2.21
3	439	102	4.30	40	176	229	52.2	4.40
4	346	73	4.74	8	158	184	53.2	19.75
5	362	77	4.70	34	42	286	79.0	1.24
6	414	88	4.70	27	75	310	74.9	2.78
7	528	114	4.63	39	92	401	75.9	2.36
8	508	102	4.98	20	106	382	75.2	5.30
9	279	61	4.57	27	60	190	68.1	2.22
10	680	115	5.91	96	88	500	73.5	0.92
11	453	92	4.92	27	47	382	84.3	1.74
12	464	88	5.27	28	84	351	75.6	3.00
13	521	93	5.60	29	71	421	80.8	2.45
14	469	94	4.99	19	84	367	78.3	4.42
15	468	107	4.37	27	86	359	76.7	3.19
16	426	99	4.30	27	64	334	78.4	2.37
17	461	99	4.67	35	101	325	70.5	2.89
18	497	139	3.59	18	108	373	75.1	6.00
19	487	123	3.96	43	102	343	70.4	2.37
20	352	81	4.35	34	74	234	66.5	2.18
21	393	85	4.62	24	109	254	64.6	4.57
22	207	39	5.31	17	82	109	62.7	4.82
23	267	51	5.18	54	54	163	61.7	1.00
24	380	80	4.75	14	94	259	68.2	6.71
25	441	83	5.31	25	70	348	78.9	2.80
TOTALS	10,513	2,237	4.70	792	2,219	7,494	71.3	2.80

SOURCE: Computed from 1819 Survey of St. John's.

Only 28.7 per cent of the population held church seats, of which 7.6 per cent of the population had seats in the Church of Scotland. This fact is significant for several reasons. First, if Chalmers refused to grant relief to members of non-Church of Scotland churches, then 21.1 per cent of the population were not entitled to relief. Second, the influence of the Church of Scotland must have been severely limited, particularly as 71.3 per cent of the population held no church seats. The figures are not too surprising in the light of the limited number of seats available. Within the parish were four churches other than the Church of Scotland, and five more were in the near proximity. The opening of St. John's probably changed the situation, as an evening congregation of parish residents was established, and they were charged lower seat rents; the Survey contains numerous references to petitions for seats for the evening service. Still, the vast majority of the parishioners were not able to obtain seats, either because of high seat rents or limited quantity of seats, or because of inability or lack of desire to attend church. Families with young children often rented only one seat, as one of the parents had to remain at home with the children. This would be reflected in the fact that 59.9 per cent of the households held at least one church seat. Seats in the Church of Scotland were held by 15.2 per cent of the households. This obviously affected the elder's tasks, as he would be welcomed in very few households during his visitations. Indeed, at least one dissenter informed Chalmers that members of St. John's session would not be allowed in his house.[9]

The Survey also contained detailed information on occupations. The largest single element of the working force was the weavers, with 411 or 18.9 per cent of the stated labour fource. The textile group contained 26.3 per cent of the labour force. Besides this, it would be safe to assume that a number of the widows, labourers, and others unspecified was engaged in the manufacturing of textiles. Hence, the well-being of the parish was obviously susceptible to variations in economic activity. The classification of weavers, widows, those unspecified, and labourers accounted for 54.4 per cent of the given jobs. As can be seen from Table IV, the types of occupations were varied, and the parish contained many elements of a self-sufficient community.

It is unfortunate that such detailed information has not been located for other parishes. Some indication of St. John's position, however, can be obtained from Cleland's *Description of the Ten Parishes*, 1820. The information is shown in Table V. St. John's, after the formation of St. James', had a population of 8,366 and 1,774 households for an average family size of 4.7. The density of St. George's and St. David's was greater with average family sizes, respectively, of 5.2 and 5.1. The average family size for Glasgow was 4.5. Hence, the density of St. John's was not much greater than that for Glasgow.

The funds for the poor in St. John's came from the church collections of the day congregation (the wealthy, non-parish residents) and of a night congregation (the poor, parish residents). The funds from the day collections were administered by the elders, and were used only for the support of the poor on the roll at the formation of the parish and for the endowment of parish schools. The elders' duties, it was believed, would quickly cease because, "... generally speaking, in Scotland pauperism implies considerable age - so that a generation of pauperism passes rapidly away".[10] Only money from the evening collection was used to support the *new* cases. The deacons were responsible for administering relief to the new cases. They had to inquire thoroughly into the circumstances and claims of every applicant. The following instructions were issued to the deacons:

TABLE IV: Summary of Occupations in St. John's Parish,
Glasgow, 1819, by Industrial Groups.

TEXTILES

Weavers	411
Spinner	47
Warper	25
Dyer	10
Tanner	10
Furrier	6
Twister	5
Cloth-capper	4
Starcher	4
Fringe-maker	1
Carder	49
Total	572

METAL INDUSTRY

Pipemaker	4
Tinsmith	2
Toolmaker	1
Coppersmith	1
Wright	46
Blacksmith	8
Ladler	1
Smith	25
Cooper	5
Total	93

CONSTRUCTION

Joiner	2
Builder	1
Sawyer	20
Mason	17
Cabinet maker	2
Slater	15
Carpenter	1
Total	58

SERVICES

Jobber	1
Barber	3
Brewer	4
Milliner	4
Confectioner	5
Servant	4
Teacher	10
Clerk	24
Beadle	3
Jeweller	3
Poulter	1
Minister	8
Publican	7
Watchman	7
Doctor	3
Baker	17
Fruiter	2
Porter	25
Hostler	8
Grocer	68
Accountant	2
Policeman	8
Total	217

OTHERS

Widows	261
Unspecified	325
Labourer	186
Unclassified	465
Total	1237

| Total Occupations | 2177 |

SOURCE: 1819 Survey at St. John's Parish.

TABLE *V*: Selected Population Statistics of Glasgow, 1820

Parish	Population			Families	Average in Family	Proportion[1] of children under 12	Proportion[1] of married males	Proportion[1] of married females	Average in Household	Proportion[1] of Servants
	Males	Female	Total							
Inner High	3571	4223	7794	1796	4.3	3.9	2.9	3.5	2.2	19.3
Tron	3291	3826	7117	1615	4.4	3.6	3.0	3.5	2.5	21.4
College	3183	3730	6913	1674	4.1	3.7	3.1	3.7	2.1	32.6
Outer High (St. Paul)	3614	4071	7685	1772	4.3	3.6	3.3	3.7	1.9	16.3
St. George's	4312	5329	9641	1863	5.2	3.3	3.2	4.0	1.5	8.8
St. David's	2723	3566	6289	1230	5.1	4.0	3.8	5.0	1.3	6.8
St. Andrew's	2663	3152	5815	1309	4.4	3.4	3.3	3.9	1.9	13.0
St. Enoch's	3220	4036	7256	1896	3.8	3.9	3.4	4.3	1.9	14.7
St. John's	4000	4366	8366	1774	4.7	3.3	3.3	3.3	2.3	33.9
St. James	3202	3718	6920	1549	4.5	3.5	3.3	3.8	2.3	18.7

(1) These values read 1: (whatever in appropriate column). Example - Servants for St. John's = 1:33.9.
    This is not a percentage figure.

SOURCE: Cleland, *Description of the Ten Parishes*, pp. 5-14.

When one applies for admittance, through his deacon, upon
our funds, the first thing to be enquired into is, if there
be any kind of work that he can yet do, so as either to
keep him altogether off, or, as to make a partial allowance
serve for his necessities. The second, what his relations
and friends are willing to do for them. The third, whether
he is a hearer in any dissenting place of worship, and
whether its Session will contribute to his relief. And,
if after these previous enquiries, it be found, that
further relief is necessary, then there must be a strict
ascertainment of his terms of residence in Glasgow, and
whether he be yet on the funds of the Town Hospital, or
is obtaining relief from any other parish.

If, upon all these points being ascertained, the deacon
of the proportion where he resides, still conceives
him an object for our assistance, he will enquire
whether a small temporary aid will meet the occasion,
and states this to the first ordinary meeting. But,
if instead of this, he conceives him a fit subject
for a regular allowance, he will receive the assistance of another deacon to complete and confirm his
enquiries, by the next ordinary meeting thereafter.
at which time, the applicant, if they still think
him a fit object, is brought before us, and received
upon the fund at such a rate of allowance as, upon all
the circumstances of the case, the meeting of deacons
shall judge proper.

Of course, pending these examinations, the deacon is
empowered to grant the same sort of discretionary aid,
that is customary in the other parishes.[11]

These instructions were amplified in a letter to Deacon Campbell

Nasmyth, dated 1st December, 1819. In the letter Chalmers described

three applications from Nasmyth's proportion and gave the appropriate

action to take on each. All should be denied relief, as they were

grounded on either a want of work or a defect of wages; this type

ought never to be granted assistance from the ordinary funds. Only

applications requesting relief because of age or bodily infirmity

should be accepted. When undertaking investigations of cases,

residence should be determined by either receipts of rents from

landlords or assertions of creditable neighbours, and evidence for

income obtained from people who furnish them with work. He reminded

Nasmyth that men were presently working in the Green for 6s. a week,

which provides an income criterion. Furthermore, if drunkenness be

a habit of the applicant, this represents an income and the application should be refused. The deserving poor are those of sound moral character.

These constitute the clearest descriptions as to how a deacon was to perform his duties. He was to be a friend and advisor to the people, a task which could be fulfilled only if he did not provide them with assistance from the session's funds. The deacon's chief function was to help the poor to help themselves, or to serve as the moral guardian of the people.

The town council's permission to establish St. John's came at a particularly bad time, for the winter of 1819-20 was one of severe economic depression for Glasgow. Especially hard hit was the cotton industry. This was important for St. John's, because, as has been stated, a large proportion of the inhabitants were weavers. The fact that Chalmers insisted, under those circumstances, in implementing his scheme is puzzling. Perhaps the explanation lies in Chalmers' character. He was a man of great self confidence, and firmly believed in the soundness of his proposals. Besides, if St. John's was able, alone, to provide for its own poor during times of great stress, there could be no better proof of the feasibility of the parochial system.

The total expenditure for the year ended 30th October, 1820 was only £317 18s. 3d., including £44 1s. 3d. spent on a soup kitchen. Chalmers later tried to capitalise on this seemingly low expenditure by stating that since the population of St. John's was ten per cent of Glasgow's population, the cost of St. John's pauperism should have been ten per cent of the assessment, or £1,400.[12] He failed, however, to state that the cost of sessional pauperism of the area formed by St. John's prior to 1819 was only £225.[13]

In 1821 the elders and deacons were so pleased with their work that they decided to exceed the original intentions of the scheme and relieve the Hospital of all paupers currently on its rolls. Chalmers did not approve of this action, as he felt the Agency was taking on an additional burden which would jeopardise the experiment. Nonetheless, on 17th May, 1821, he requested a list of out-pensioners and inmates of the Hospital who were residents within the parish of St. John's. He also informed the Hospital directors that steps were in progress for placing such persons on the funds of St. John's. This action was succeeded by a letter from Robert Brown, an elder at St. John's, dated 7th January, 1822, to the Hospital directors. In the letter Mr Brown stated that the session was now ready to relieve the Hospital of these cases. They were to remain in the Hospital, and, provided they received the average Hospital allowance, St. John's would not interfere with their management. Mr Brown also stated that if the collections at St. John's suffered a serious decrease, the arrangement might have to be ended.

Dr Chalmers, having left Glasgow in November, 1823 to assume the Chair of Moral Philosophy at St. Andrew's, later wrote that, during his stay at St. John's,

> The whole number of regular paupers who have been admitted on the parochial funds of St. John's, for three years and nine months, is twenty, at a monthly expense of £5 10s. 6d. and a yearly expense of £66 6s. during which period there has not one been sent to the Town Hospital, or made chargeable in any way, on the fund by assessment.[14]

The number admitted on the grounds of general indigence was thirteen (monthly expense of £2 13s. 4d.); the number admitted on the grounds of extraordinary and hopeless disease was two, one lunatic and one deaf and dumb individual for a monthly expense of £1 4s. 8d.; the number admitted on the grounds of necessity springing from crime was five, two illegitimate children and three families of runaway husbands for a monthly expense of £1 12s. 6d. Chalmers felt that only those of the first group were the proper recipients of relief; the second group should be cared for by publicly supported institutions and the third group should not receive relief. But he failed to present an accurate picture; St. John's was indeed sending cases to the Town's Hospital. Moreover, the session refused to grant aid to any person who had previously received relief, regardless of its source. This policy is clearly evident from two items contained in the Chalmers' Papers. The first is a letter to Chalmers from William Sym, clerk to the weekly Committee of the Town's Hospital, dated 26th October, 1819.

> Regarding the principle assumed and intended to be acted upon by Dr Chalmers and his Session, namely that a person who has at any time received a Temporary Supply from the Charitable Funds of any parish, becomes in all time subsequent inseparably attached to that parish in so far as a right to charity is concerned - and that that person cannot obtain a legal claim to Support from any other parish at any after period however distant, and however changed his circumstances may have been in the outcoming period. This principle the Committee do not understand to be correct in Law and know it to be contrary to the practices of all neighbouring parishes.
>
> The Committee conceive that it would be equally unwarrantable and more inequitable for the Session of St. John's to refuse aid to every poor person who may be long resident in that ???, on the Sole ground that they had at some time received even a Small Temporary Supply from Managers of the Town's Hospital the more especially as the poor part of the population of that parish is so numerous, and their circumstances so much subject to change.
>
> The Committee further conceive that if the Session of St. John's go upon the data they propose they will be able to guard their funds very effectually as it is believed that on investigation it will be found that by far the greater number of the lower class in that parish have at some time or other received aid in some shape from the legal charitable funds of the City.

The second piece of evidence of inaccuracy in Chalmers' picture is an undated [1820?] note to himself.

> In Mr McVeys proportion a woman blind in years, and received 1/6 a week several years from the Hospital, and 3/- a month from the female Society. The latter Society have withdrawn their support on the plan that I was to take on all their cases. Mr McVey on being told of it by the woman referred her to the Town Hospital for the necessary ??? - they sent her back to him on the plan that I was to support all the poor of my parish. And not till after a good deal of counter statements and altercations at the Hospital between two of my people and the Committee was the woman restated upon their funds.

Besides these cases, all cases of medical relief were referred to the Hospital.[15] Chalmers' careful and arbitrary definition of the classes eligible for relief artificially reduced the problem as concerned and measured in St. John's parish, the harshness of his measures falling on those less able to bear them.

Dr. Patrick MacFarlan was appointed to replace Chalmers as minister. His stay at St. John's was short, for eighteen months later, the town council appointed him to the vacant charge of St. Enoch's. Dr. Thomas Brown became minister in 1826. He continued in that capacity for the remainder of the period under consideration. Unfortunately, events during this period are largely unknown. As one would expect, the session minutes for St. John's contain few entries relative to poor relief. It is clear that the foundling children were boarded out with respectable people, with an elder checking on them once a month to ensure that they were properly fed, clothed, and instructed in religious principles. On 10th December, 1827, a decision was made to arrange for

> raising the funds necessary to pay the Salaries of the
> Parochial Teachers which had hitherto been paid from the
> Collections for the poor - but which collections it was
> considered proper to relieve if possible from that
> burden in time coming.[16]

It was agreed to have two collections annually, both in the Church and the Chapel of Ease, and that that intention be stated from the pulpit on the previous Sunday. All costs of educating orphans and foundling children were to come from these collections. On 7th September, 1832, the St. John's Kirk Session Minutes report that an extraordinary collection for the poor was made, because of the great additional burden imposed by a severe epidemic leaving orphaned children in its wake, and because the funds had been considerably affected by the church's closure for repairs during several weeks.

The events leading to the end of the experiment are clearly stated in the Hospital minutes. On 20th November, 1832, a communication was received from Robert Dalglish, former Lord Provost recommending the liquidation from the funds of the Hospital of a claim for £11 5s. 4d. expended by the deacons of St. John's on extraordinary aid to persons and families suffering from typhus fever. This request was granted, as an agreement with the Hospital in 1819 stated that the parish could draw on the Hospital funds for any unusual expenditure. This was the first time they drew from the Hospital. The next mention was on 29th March, 1836, when a delegation from St. John's called upon the Weekly Committee to report the sad state of their funds and to remind the Committee of the agreements made between the session and the directors in 1822, which have previously been stated. The Weekly Committee agreed to submit the session's petition to the directors, who appointed a committee to examine the claims. This committee reported on 1st April, 1836, that it would be contrary to law to meet the claim for aid by the session on the basis of accumulated arrears of the last fourteen years on a particular class of paupers. But if

> ... the Session be enabled to shew that from recent claims
> of unusual magnitude, they have been involved in debt which
> they have not the means of discharging, the Committee would
> recommend the claim to the favourable consideration of the
> Directors.[17]

This statement received the following response from William Buchanan dated 28th April, 1836:

> The Committee of St. John's Session having considered the
> Minutes of the Committee of the Town's Hospital, of date
> 1 Current, and advised with St. John's Session, beg leave
> to state that their debt has arisen principally since
> 1832 - that a principal cause has been the increase of
> expenditure consequent upon the cholera which raged in
> 1832 followed by Typhus Fever in 1833, and from the
> unlooked for four great extent of Lunatic cases
> principally augmented in 1834 and 1835. This Committee
> respectfully remind the Committee of the Town's Hospital,
> that their application is for reimbursement of the
> £461 duly verified by Mr Hill, as actually paid to the
> Hospital, under the Second or Supplementary undertaking
> of 1820.[18]

This represented a convenient rewording of the original petition which claimed that the balance against the session had arisen because of payments to the Town's Hospital for support of the poor on the Hospital's rolls at the formation of the parish. As a result of this sacrifice of principles, the directors agreed to pay St. John's the amount requested and expressed their hope that the session would be able to carry on as before. But on 21st May, 1836, a directive was received from the town council that the £461 was not to be paid to St. John's until acted on by the council, which also demanded the documents and extracts of the proceedings relative to the application from the session. The directors voted to ignore this directive on the grounds that the council had delegated their responsibility to the poor to the directors. Finally, on 3rd October, 1837, the session reported that the state of their funds was such that they needed assistance from the Hospital on the same grounds as the other nine parishes. The directors agreed to the request and stated that all persons receiving more than 5s. per month would be placed on the Hospital rolls, as would all orphans, deserted children, and lunatics. With this decision, the eighteen year experiment came to an end.

After leaving the parish, Chalmers kept in close contact with events there. In his last article on the experiment written in 1841, he offered several reasons for the system's failure. He felt it was a success if the expenditure for religious and educational objects was not taken into account. This would be true. However, since education played such a crucial role in the parochial system, it does not seem reasonable to exclude the expenditure when evaluating the system. He also felt that the parish should never have undertaken the obligation to support its poor in the Town's Hospital. Finally, he stated that the system was doomed to failure as long as the magistrates refused to impose a law of settlement between the parishes within Glasgow, and as long as they refused to exempt the inhabitants of St. John's from paying the assessment.[19] Both of these demands were unrealistic. Since Glasgow, for the purposes of civil law, was one parish, a law of settlement could not be established between the *quoad sacra* parishes. The second demand should have had no influence on the system, as most of the residents of the parish did not have enough means to be assessed. The largest percentage of St. John's income came from the wealthy, non-resident members of the congregation.

Chalmers was right in one respect; the experiment was doomed to failure. This can be seen clearly from Table VI. This abstract of the treasurer's accounts has been selected, as it agrees with manuscript abstracts found in the Chalmers' Papers for the years 1820-1823. It also correctly reflects the categories of expenditure one would expect to find included in the Chalmerian parochial system. One fact is immediately clear; income was greater than expenditure only for the years 1820, 1821, 1822, and 1824; from 1825 until 1833, the session had to receive some form of outside help. Could this be the secret subsidies referred to by his critics, J. H. Burton, Andrew Ranken, and W. P. Alison.[20] The Table also illustrates that the allusion, addressed to the directors of the Town's Hospital, to the session's financial difficulties arising in 1832 because of the cholera epidemic was not true. The session's financial difficulties were a long-term matter, arising because of faulty managerial decisions and an over-zealous agency. If the session had not under-taken the relief of the cases in the Town's Hospital, they would have had a balance in their favour of £146 instead of a deficit. The blame cannot be placed on expenditure for education and the relief of paupers not considered to be proper objects of parochial relief, since these expenses represented managerial decisions and correctly reflect the fact that they had to be made. If St. John's had been a rural parish, it would have been legally responsible for the type of expenditure given in the Table.

TABLE VI:

St. John's Parish, Glasgow: Abstract from Treasurer's Accounts of Income and Expenditure from 1 October 1819 to 1 October 1833.[1]

Years	INCOME				EXPENDITURE									
	No. of Regular and Occasional Sessional Poor[2]	Collections at Church and Chapel Doors	General Session Fund and Sundries	Total Income	Paid to Regular Session Poor[3]	Paid to Occasional Poor	Foundlings Deserted Children etc.	Lunatic Paupers	Coffins and Funeral Expenses[4]	Expenses of Parochial Schools	Religious and Charitable Institutions	Church Officers and Sundries	Total Expenditure	Net Balance
	1	2	3	4	5	6	7	8	9	10	11	12	13	14
	£	£	£	£	£	£	£	£	£	£	£	£	£	£
1820	117	713	22	735	222				95	154	168	44	683	52
1821	113	734	25	759	193			4	10	51	269	16	543	216
1822	78	739	54	793	149			8	13	107	298	26	60	192
1823	74	570	39	609	264	8	1	4	10	581	134	28	1,022[5]	-413
1824	92	535	172	707	201	11	25	6	11	207	113	38	609	98
1825	110	422	28	450	169	9	19	9	7	80	161	45	501	-51
1826	160	465	46	511	228	13	53	29	6	72	74	80	551	-40
1827	165	535	60	595	279	8	54	17	22	72	173	65	695	-100
1828	88	524	81	605	287	26	88	20	11	85	109	41	636	-31
1829	89	499	43	542	176	21	127	41	23	103	102	72	652	-110
1830	83	469	43	512	187		86	41	13		21	49	521	-9

(continued overleaf).

TABLE VI (continued)

Years	INCOME				EXPENDITURE									
	No. of Regular and Occasional Sessional Poor[2]	Collections at Church and Chapel Doors	General Session Fund and Sundries	Total Income	Paid to Regular Session Poor[3]	Paid to Occasional Poor	Foundlings Deserted Children etc.	Lunatic Paupers	Coffins and Funeral Expenses[4]	Expenses of Parochial Schools	Religious and Charitable Institutions	Church Officers and Sundries	Total Expenditure	Net Balance
	1	2	3	4	5	6	7	8	9	10	11	12	13	14
1831	83	492	43	535	182	25	69	30	21	123	56	62	568	-33
1832	82	561	45	606	187	28	107	30	24	78	84	69	607	-1
1833	92	543	41	584	205	32	117	21	10	95	106	53	639	-55
Totals		7,801	742	8,543	2,929	181	746	260	276	1,880	1,868	688	8,287	-285

[1] James Cleland, *Letter to his Grace the Duke of Hamilton and Brandon respecting parochial register of Scotland* (Glasgow 1834) p. 40.

[2] For years 1820–1827 all classes of paupers are included. For years 1828–1833 the numbers of foundlings, orphans, deserted children, lunatics and occasional paupers are not included.

[3] Includes payments to Town Hospital.

[4] In 1820 about £70 was expended in providing Mortcloths for the use of the Parish.

[5] Includes £500 invested in Corporation funds for an endowment of £25 per annum to pay school master.

SOURCES: Cleland, James. *Letter to His Grace the Duke of Hamilton*, p. 40.

Perhaps Chalmers could foresee impending difficulties; hence, his rather untimely exit in 1823. His appointment to the Chair at St. Andrew's was not announced until his election to the Chair.[21] In announcing his decision to leave, he informed his Agency that the move was necessary because of his health.[22] This was the first reference to a poor state of health at this period of his life. The Agency was shocked. In a letter to Chalmers on 20th January, 1823, William Collins stated "In general, they (the elders and deacons) could have wished you had remained a year or two longer until your Parochial measures had been more fully matured".[23] It is evident in a letter from Harry Rainy that the experiment relied heavily on Chalmers. Rainy stated that the circumstances of the Agency were not on as harmonious a footing as could be wished, and that the Church was poorly attended, with collections consequently considerably decreased.[24]

The only successful undertaking by Chalmers at St. John's was in the area of education.

> Within two years from the commencement of his ministry
> four efficient teachers, each endowed to the extent
> of twenty-five pounds per annum, were educating 419
> scholars; and when he left Glasgow in 1823 other
> school buildings were in process of erection capable
> of accommodating 374 additional pupils; so that the
> fruit of four years' labour was the leaving behind
> him the means and facilities for giving at a very
> moderate rate a superior education to no less than
> 793 children out of a population of 10,000 souls.[25]

As for the allusion to secret subsidies, surely one should not criticise the system on the grounds that wealthy persons provided donations to the poor in order to keep them off the rolls. After all this function was one of Chalmers' four fountains, and under the parochial system everything should be done to prevent a person from suffering the moral degradation of receiving aid from the sessional funds. Moreover, Chalmers never tried to hide the fact that the wealthy were making substantial donations to the poor. Campbell Nasmyth in his testimony before the 1844 Commission when asked the

question, "And some of them [the deacons] tried to get work for the
applicants?" responded,

> Yes; wherever I could I used my influence; and even
> although I did not know personally the persons to whom
> I applied, I stated to them in writing, or otherwise,
> that the poor person for whom I sought work was deserv-
> ing, honest, and well disposed, and that it might be
> safe to give them work.[26]

Chalmers claimed that he relieved from his own resources [£20] all
the cases in Archibald Newbegging's proportion in 1819-1820. These
subsidies, however, could be criticised on the grounds that their
extent and necessity were never made known. Apparently, the system
was able to survive only because of such subsidies. Without this
information, Chalmers' statements on St. John's are misleading.

Evidence has been presented which indicates that the experiment
was not financially successful. But another aspect of the system
needs to be examined: Chalmers argued that the system of independent
management saved Glasgow a substantial amount, therefore permitting
a reduction in the assessments. Was this claim warranted? Although
the evidence is extremely scanty, such as it is indicates that the
experiment was costly to Glasgow. First, using Chalmers' own figures,
we learn that in 1823, St. John's cost of maintaining its poor in the
Town's Hospital was only £90. In the same year the assessment for
Glasgow was £8,561, of which the inhabitants of St. John's paid
£140. As £90 is only one per cent of the assessment, this could not
be considered a substantial saving to Glasgow. Furthermore, by an
agreement made in 1819, as the poor from St. John's in the Hospital
died, a proportional sum from the *assessment* was to be remitted to
the parish.[27]

Secondly, the General Session foresaw difficulties. At their
meeting of 2nd September, 1819, they proposed to allocate the expected
collections among the nine parishes so that the average allowance per
pauper would be 2/9. But if Dr. Chalmers were to

> ... retain his Collections at £8 a week, or £416, and
> consequently parochial poor 125 withdrawn, the other
> parishes would only have monthly allowances per pauper
> of 2/6. But if Dr. Chalmers will give up £184 3s. 6d.
> of his collections to the Common Funds of the Session
> this will raise the whole to 2/9.[28]

Chalmers would not agree to this proposal, hence on 7th October, 1819,

the General Session resigned its management of the sessional poor,

but after negotiation with the town council they agreed to continue

until 15th February, 1821. This action complicated the system of

management in Glasgow; now, each session had to negotiate separately

with the Town's Hospital for funds. Of the ten parishes only four

initially drew upon the Hospital's funds; the other six decided to

rely on their own collections. However, by 1832 all parishes except

St. John's were drawing from the Hospital. St. George's parish on

5th February, 1821, decided to yield to the majority opinion and

distribute from their own collections. They expressed the feeling,

however, that Glasgow needed some central court, such as the General

Session, to supervise the distribution of funds in order to preserve

a uniformity in distribution, and that Glasgow was a parish *quoad*

civilia and therefore each separate parish within the City could not

legally act on its own.

Thirdly, the Chalmerian system forced the assessments in Glasgow

to be greater than they would have been under the former system. It

must be remembered that, prior to the resignation of the General

Session, each session gave its collections to the General Session,

who redistributed the amount to the various parishes in proportion

to the number on their rolls. Any deficiency in required amounts

was to be made up by the Town's Hospital. After the resignation of

the General Session each parish retained its collections. Thus, any

balance in its funds would remain with the parish and would be lost

to the system, hence it could not be used to help to off-set the

deficits of the other parishes. The total balances in hand from

church door collections in all Glasgow parishes on 1st November, 1822,
were £1,195 3s. 6½d. Moreover, over one-half of this balance, or
£604, was in the hands of St. John's. As the other parishes had
deficits of £687, the amount of the assessment for Glasgow had to be
greater by the £687. Thus, the system could not have been considered
as creating savings to Glasgow.

In conclusion, it does not seem possible to state that the
experiment was a success in terms of its effect on the other parishes.
Besides increasing the cost of pauperism in Glasgow, it created a
certain chaos by eliminating the important element of uniformity in
the system. The parochial system was never adopted on a large scale
by those parishes that had resorted to an assessment. Chalmers
himself stated that he did not feel sorry about the abandonment of the
system at St. John's, as the deacons would not have any impetus to
work on what was considered an experiment unlikely to be adopted.[29]
His greatest opponent, W. P. Alison stated, with respect to a
voluntary system being established, that Chalmers' own statements
show its impracticability when he confessed that his "Contest of
twenty-five years with public functionaries has been weary and
ineffectual" and that no other parish in Glasgow had followed his
example.[30] Perhaps the system was not adopted elsewhere because it
was an attempt to reverse the social impact of industrialisation. It
was therefore bound to fail because of the new tide of social
conscience that was sweeping Britain. The following comments by a
contemporary, Sheriff Archibald Alison, provide an excellent
evaluation of Chalmers' attitudes on poor relief:

> His ideas about the management of the poor were those
> of benevolent and visionary rather than a practical and
> sagacious man: they pre-supposed a greater amount of
> talent in the minister, and zeal in his associates,
> than is to be expected from the average of men.[31]

In spite of its failure and its attempt to turn back the clock,
the system embodied several important and surprising innovations.

First, it emphasised that the problems of poverty could be solved only by attacking the source of poverty, not by attempting to relieve poverty; treating the symptoms will only disguise and perpetuate the problems of poverty. Second, if an over-supply of labour existed in an industry, the superfluous workers should, at public expense, be fitted out for other jobs. Finally, Chalmers developed the important principle of 'locality': the poor should be helped at the local level by individuals familiar with their needs; the social worker should be viewed as an understanding friend.

---

* Sections of this Chapter are from R. A. Cage and E. O. A. Checkland, "Thomas Chalmers and Urban Poverty: The St. John's Parish Experiment in Glasgow, 1819-1837", in *Philosophical Journal*, vol. 13, No. 1, Spring, 1976.

1. Chalmers, *Political Economy*, n.d., p. 254.

2. Chalmers, *Christian and Civic Economy*, 1823, vol. 2, p. 51.

3. Chalmers, *Christian and Civic Economy*, 1823, vol. 2, p. 99.

4. Chalmers, *Sermons*, 1823, p. 376.

5. A detailed description of this system appears in Chapter 3.

6. Chalmers, *Christian and Civic Economy*, 1823, vol. 2, p. 100.

7. Chalmers, *Christian and Civic Economy*, 1823, vol. 2, p. 116.

8. The manuscript was entitled "Statistical, Moral, and Educational Survey of St. John's Parish, Glasgow; for the year 1819", and "To the Rev. Dr. Chalmers, this Survey is respectfully presented by the Elders, Deacons, and Sabbath School Teachers, of St. John's Parish, Glasgow." Chalmers' Papers, New College Library, Edinburgh.

9. Chalmers' Papers, Letter from George Martin, 12th October, 1819.

10. Chalmers, *Christian and Civic Economy*, 1823, vol. 2, p. 144.

11. Chalmers, *Christian and Civic Economy*, 1823, vol. 2, pp. 151-52.

12. Chalmers, *On the Sufficiency*, 1841, p. 100. It should be noted that Chalmers never stated that he decreased the cost of pauperism in St. John's from £1,400 to £280, as Hanna claims. Hanna, *Life of Chalmers*, vol. 2, p. 297.

13. Glasgow General Session Minutes, Mitchell Library.

14. Chalmers, *Last Eight Years*, 1823, p. 15.

110.

15. Chalmers' Papers, note to himself, 16th May, 1823.

16. St. John's KSM, 10th December, 1827.

17. Town's Hospital Minutes, 1st April, 1836.

18. Town's Hospital Minutes, 28th April, 1836.

19. Chalmers, *On the Sufficiency*, 1841, pp. 135-37.

20. Burton stated in "Poor Laws and Pauperism in Scotland", in *Westminster Review*, 1841, p. 23, that "We admit that it is not unlikely that it would be found, on inquiry, that the poor of St. John's did obtain more of the comforts of life than their neighbours, but if they did so, it was from circumstances which the friends of the scheme would keep in the background. The project required the aid of several respectable citizens to act in the capacity of deacons, and administer the fund. These consisted of the most wealthy citizens of all parts of the town. They were men chosen out and distinguished, and a good deal was expected of them. It was a pet scheme, in short, of the aristocracy of Glasgow, who were bound to come in personal contact with the poor of a small section of the city. The influence of these gentlemen, in the way of procuring employment, and in various other forms, was thus in a manner at the service of their clients; we have heard, too that their purses were frequently appealed to, and that the honour was a somewhat expensive one."

21. Chalmers' Papers, Letter from Francis Nicoll, St. Andrew's, 11th January, 1823.

22. Chalmers' Papers, 20th January, 1823.

23. Chalmers' Papers, Letter from William Collins, 20th January, 1823.

24. Chalmers' Papers, Letter from Harry Rainy, 28th February, 1824.

25. Hanna, *Life of Chalmers*, 1832, vol. 2, p. 236.

26. *1844 Report*, vol. 1, p. 350.

27. St. John's Session. *Statement from the Session of St. John's Parish, Glasgow to the Directors of the Town's Hospital, in Regard to the Management of Their Poor* (1836).

28. GSM, 2nd September, 1819.

29. Chalmers, *On the Sufficiency*, 1841, p. 145.

30. Alison, *Reply to Dr. Chalmers' Objections*, 1841, p. 3.

31. Lady Jane Alison, 1883, p. 448.

As in England, large scale disagreement about the operation of the
poor laws occurred only after 1815. The war years (1795-1815) caused
both the number of paupers and expenditure on them to increase
dramatically, resulting in the introduction of assessments and an
increase in the rates. By tracing the course of discontent, an
understanding of the reasons for changing the law in 1845 can be
obtained.

Isolated cases of discontent periodically occurred in Scotland
throughout the period. Not surprisingly urban areas, particularly
Glasgow, were the main centres. An early example was dated 1785 and
opened with the statement: "He that oppresseth the Poor, reproacheth
his Maker".[1] The author's purpose was to criticise the views of a
collection of letters by a writer calling himself 'A Citizen', who
claimed that individuals receiving public assistance should descend
at least one step below the station he held during periods of health
and industry.[2] The protagonist of the poor believed these views to
be irrelevant, as the allowances to the poor were far from sufficient.
A fellow anonymous author was opposed to a legal assessment, but he
was also hostile to any voluntary system not based upon church
collections. It was only in a church that "Habit closes the grudging
eye of avarice; and vanity, in the presence of the church where there
are so many spectators to note a close-fisted Christian, comes forward
as a friendly auxiliary to virture". Ironically, a family of
Christians ". . . bestow this sum cheerfully, and never think more
of it".[3] Individuals who desert the Church, however, and are
approached at the end of the year feel that the sums asked of them
are unjustly high. Finally, considering parochial relief in Glasgow,
one writer criticised the administrators and low relief payments.
". . . the quantum of which too frequently corresponds with the
favourable or unfavourable representation of their Elders, and which

is at best by no means sufficient for supporting life".[4]

A. *The 1818 Report*

At the end of the Napoleonic Wars, largely as a result of the increased number of paupers and expenditure on them the English were seriously challenging the validity of their poor laws and were looking with envious eyes at the Scottish system. In order to evaluate the impact of differing types of legislation, the Select Committee on the English Poor Law early in 1817 asked the General Assembly of the Church of Scotland to undertake a study of the Scottish poor law. The General Assembly agreed in May of that year, appointing a sub-committee with George H. Baird, Principal of Edinburgh University, as convener and presenting the results to the Select Committee the following May. To accomplish their task, the sub-committee compiled a set of queries and sent them to each parish minister of the Church of Scotland, receiving back 717 completed returns, representing seventy-eight per cent of Scotland's parishes. The task of compiling and analysing the returns was done by a single individual. Little wonder then that mistakes in data presentation were later admitted, and a supplementary Report issued in 1820 giving corrections. The conclusions, however, were not modified, being representative of the existing political and social conditions.

The Report had a more extensive data base than the English Report of 1817 and, indeed, than that of 1834. There is no problem of defining a statistical sample, as nearly all the Scottish parishes are represented. Moreover, it is possible to determine which parishes did not submit returns, thus avoiding a complaint Blaug registered against the 1824 *Report of the Select Committee on Labourers' Wages*.[5] Other complaints which Blaug expressed against the 1834 English Report[6] are not applicable to the Scottish Report, as the questionnaires were analysed and reduced to summary form,

though many important questions were, seemingly, overlooked. The
summary tables presented only information on church collections,
assessments, expenditure, and number of poor, thus eliminating a vast
quantity of other useful information. The questions were clearer and
better designed than those for the English Report of 1834, though it
is evident from the summary data that confusion existed in the answers,
reflecting, perhaps, more the haphazard manner in which records were
kept rather than any weakness in the form of the questions. As the
original returns could not be located, one must rely on the data
abstracts which appear in the published Report. The information was
arranged by parish according to synod and presbytery and included for
each parish the population in 1811, the average funds for the poor
for 1808-17 including contributions by the heritors, amount of annual
assessments, and the average annual number of paupers for 1808-17,
including both those regularly and occasionally on the poor's roll.
The conclusions of the Report purport to be based on abridged answers
to the forty queries.

   The Report's main theme was to stress the evils of legal assessment, a reiteration of the basic Scottish tenet that a legal assessment was necessary only if the voluntary sources of funds were
insufficient. Moreover, the assessment was to be conceived only as
a supplement to the voluntary contributions, the power to determine
the amount resting with the persons liable to its payment. The Report
emphasises the "goodness" of this approach for it "... has long
contributed so largely to the industry and comfort of the poor,
without producing any general injurious oppression on the rich."[7]
The committee members' opinions were clarified and strengthened at a
a later point, emphasising that,

> ... they do not mean to enter into any general reasonings,
> respecting the various bearings of assessments on national
> policy and morals, or the relative interests of the

rich and of the poor; but they cannot avoid expressing
their conviction, that the full and accurate details
furnished by the numerous returns from the ministers of
parishes that are assessed, have enabled them to produce
an extent and kind of evidence more conclusive than has
ever been collected hitherto in Scotland, not only of
the pernicious tendency in general of these compulsatory
[sic] taxations, but of their having already made a
progress in this country, which ought to excite the
alarm of all who take an interest in its welfare.[8]

The Report next examined the progressive rise in assessments,

illustrating how the amounts increased substantially over the period

1808-1817, and concluding that the increase was due to a

... decisive and striking practical proof, that
compulsory assessments will soon be found unavoidable,
wherever the feelings of the lower classes become
habituated to the view of the claims made, and allowances received under them elsewhere.[9]

It further argued that the imposition of assessments caused church

collections to decrease. The Report fails to consider the proposition

that legal assessments were introduced only if the voluntary sources

of funds were insufficient to meet the demands placed upon them. The

number of people demanding or requiring help increased during the

Napoleonic Wars since families of soldiers were supported by the

parishes. In addition absenteeism by landlords led to a falling off

of church door collections, and the large scale movement of rural

population to urban areas, without any new church building led to a

lowering of church attendance, and therefore of church collections,

in urban areas. Thus it seems that assessments were augmented

because of worsening economic conditions; they did not cause a drop

in church collections, as the Report contends.

The Report repeatedly argues that the introduction of a legal

assessment caused the numbers on the rolls to multiply, for all moral

constraint was removed. Introduce a legal assessment, and the poor

demand relief as a right, the shame of applying for it will be

effaced. An assessment "... multiplies the number of paupers, by

debasing and corrupting one class of the population, and leading to

to an extravagant expenditure in supporting them, it unjustly and
unnecessarily oppresses the other".[10] Yet the available evidence does
not support this conclusion, as the population of the unassessed
parishes was nearly twice that of the assessed (640,015 and 339,879
respectively), but the number of paupers in the unassessed was more
than twice that of the assessed 19,786 and 8,385 respectively).

The Report correctly stated that paupers rarely received full
support from the parish allowance, except in a few cases of friendless
lunatics and foundlings. In determining the amount of the allowances,
real poverty was always relieved, but not to the full extent of need.
The amount and kind of allowance bestowed was influenced by the
applicant's character and known habits. As the Scottish poor law
directed that the amount of relief should be sufficient to provide
the pauper with the means of subsistence, without having to resort
to begging, the relief prescribed by the law exceeded that actually
awarded and was a reflection of the prevailing philosophy of the
administrators that the amount of relief received should be viewed
as a supplement to other sources of income.

On the important question of removal the Report presents a half-
truth, arguing that there was never an instance of removal of a
pauper from one parish to another involuntarily or by legal means.
Furthermore, this practice of not removing an individual after he
became chargeable to public charity was stated to be beneficial to
the industrial development of Scotland, by permitting free circulation
of the labour force.[11] The beneficial nature of this practice is
uncertain if, as reputedly was the case, only the old, orphaned, and
disabled were relieved. The positive effects of a mobile labour
force cannot be denied, but the Report's presentation is over-
simplified. Paupers were indeed not sent back to their place of
settlement. But ample evidence exists that *poor* persons were removed
from a parish before they could acquire a three years residence. The

116.

instrument of removal was not, however, provided by the poor law as such, but by zealous sheriffs who soon evicted persons who did not possess certificates from their parish of settlement attesting to their moral character and ability to support themselves.[12]

Important insights can be gained by a detailed examination of data contained in the Report and reproduced on a county basis in Table VII. Several additional computations were made, so it is possible to determine by county the level of total expenditure on relief, the expenditure per pauper, the expenditure per head of population, and the percentage of the population who were paupers. Though these categories were examined in the Report, the data were never systematically presented, the authors relying on selected conclusions. As can be seen, the average annual level of total expenditure per county for the whole of Scotland during the ten years preceding 1818 was £130 3s. 2d. The highest was in Edinburgh and amounted to £564 16s. 0d., whereas the lowest was £14 8s. 9d. in Orkney. Generally, the level of total expenditure was highest in those counties with industrial centres and areas of high population densities. Expenditure per pauper was substantially higher in the Borders than elsewhere, the average annual amount for Roxburgh being £6 19s. 10d. The figure for the areas of northern and western Scotland exhibits a remarkably low level of assistance, being only 14s. 4d., and if the counties of Argyle and Bute are excluded, the figure drops to about 9s. per pauper per year. Clearly, paupers in the northern portions of Scotland were receiving other forms of assistance. The figures for expenditure per head of population illustrate the same relationships between regions as those for expenditure per pauper. The amount for the Southern Uplands was higher than the national average. Nonetheless, it cannot be claimed that the assessed parishes were over-generous in providing relief when the annual cost of relief per person was less than two shillings a year.

TABLE VII: Selected annual means for total expenditure, expenditure per pauper, expenditure per head of population, and paupers as a percentage of population by county, 1818 and 1839.

County	1818 Expenditure £	s.	d.	Exp/pauper £	s.	d.	Exp/head £	s.	d.	% of pop. who are paupers	1839 Expenditure £	s.	d.	Exp/pauper £	s.	d.	Exp/head £	s.	d.	% of pop. who are paupers	% of assessed parishes 1818	% of assessed parishes 1839
Orkney	14	8	9	0	8	3	0	0	1	2.70	15	7	7	0	6	9	0	0	1	3.93	0.00	0.00
Caithness	27	9	0	0	6	10	0	0	2	3.80	39	18	9	0	8	8	0	0	2	3.13	0.00	0.00
Sutherland	21	7	3	0	10	4	0	0	1	3.37	27	6	10	0	7	2	0	0	3	5.38	0.00	0.00
Ross and Cromarty	31	3	2	0	9	9	0	0	2	3.74	31	8	3	0	7	8	0	0	2	3.69	0.00	0.00
Inverness	40	5	2	0	12	4	0	0	2	2.48	26	16	10	0	8	9	0	0	1	2.95	0.00	0.00
Argyle	37	4	0	1	1	9	0	0	3	1.65	66	1	10	1	5	6	0	0	8	2.60	0.00	5.13
Bute	74	2	8	2	3	9	0	0	9	1.84	97	12	6	1	4	6	0	0	6	2.26	0.00	0.00
Nairn	26	13	0	0	10	7	0	0	2	3.75	34	1	7	0	9	6	0	0	3	4.07	0.00	0.00
Elgin	43	6	10	0	17	10	0	0	6	3.11	60	13	9	0	16	0	0	0	8	3.87	0.00	0.00
Banff	60	10	10	1	9	2	0	0	9	2.91	84	6	8	1	7	9	0	0	9	3.17	0.00	0.00
Aberdeen	64	19	9	2	1	0	0	0	9	2.38	121	15	6	1	16	6	0	0	9	2.76	0.00	1.12
Kincardine	63	15	9	2	0	1	0	0	10	2.58	98	10	6	1	19	6	0	0	9	3.02	0.00	4.76
Forfar	128	1	10	2	18	6	0	0	10	2.31	204	11	0	3	3	9	0	1	2	2.36	5.45	10.91
Perth	117	2	6	3	7	0	0	0	9	1.67	121	8	6	2	18	0	0	1	2	2.34	13.92	22.78
Fife	84	5	1	3	2	4	0	1	0	2.05	113	11	0	2	11	4	0	1	0	2.49	12.70	14.30
Kinross	52	18	0	3	17	8	0	0	11	1.31	55	7	0	2	12	4	0	0	8	1.53	0.00	0.00
Clackmannan	221	15	0	2	19	2	0	0	1	2.17	250	15	8	2	7	6	0	0	10	2.19	16.67	16.67
Linlithgow	87	5	4	3	8	9	0	0	2	2.04	135	16	3	3	15	5	0	0	6	2.90	14.44	21.30
Edinburgh	564	16	0	4	8	4	0	1	6	2.23	676	8	9	3	7	8	0	1	7	2.71	56.25	71.87
Haddington	155	2	0	4	12	3	0	0	2	2.56	164	15	1	3	9	9	0	2	0	3.05	50.00	54.16

(continued overleaf)

TABLE VII: (Continued)

County	1818 Expenditure £	s.	d.	Exp/pauper £	s.	d.	Exp/head £	s.	d.	% of pop. who are paupers	1839 Expenditure £	s.	d.	Exp/pauper £	s.	d.	Exp/head £	s.	d.	% of pop. who are paupers	% of assessed parishes 1818	1839
Stirling	128	16	6	4	11	6	0	1	1	1.42	141	1	6	2	7	7	0	0	10	1.97	11.54	19.23
Dumbarton	92	8	6	3	4	4	0	0	9	1.51	152	0	0	2	15	9	0	1	0	1.86	0.00	16.67
Renfrew	523	8	0	3	19	7	0	1	2	1.67	540	5	8	3	3	8	0	1	1	2.53	31.56	47.78
Lanark	417	15	9	4	9	2	0	1	0	1.57	411	7	0	2	12	3	0	1	1	2.31	29.27	36.10
Ayr	126	18	7	4	2	11	0	1	0	1.51	177	6	9	2	6	9	0	1	0	2.73	17.40	32.61
Berwick	146	10	10	5	7	0	0	2	8	2.84	168	3	7	3	17	0	0	2	9	3.76	48.48	48.48
Peebles	58	4	1	5	3	0	0	1	7	1.90	64	17	9	4	12	6	0	1	9	2.38	26.67	33.33
Selkirk	122	14	6	5	14	5	0	2	6	2.28	124	15	8	4	0	0	0	0	11	2.42	55.56	55.56
Roxburgh	208	19	9	6	19	10	0	3	4	2.80	211	16	0	3	15	6	0	2	7	3.82	51.11	51.11
Dumfries	88	17	3	2	14	6	0	1	0	1.93	135	13	2	2	10	5	0	1	4	2.89	16.28	37.21
Kirkcudbright	47	10	8	2	16	8	0	0	10	1.67	83	13	0	2	9	0	0	1	2	3.19	00.00	10.60
Wigton	55	2	9	2	3	3	0	0	9	1.64	99	13	2	2	2	8	0	0	10	2.50	00.00	00.00
Scotland	130	3	2	3	0	4	0	1	0	2.21	159	2	8	2	6	9	0	1	1	2.85	14.49	20.22

SOURCE: Computed from data contained in 1818 and 1839 Reports.

117.

Even that amount, however, was large when compared with the one and two pence per year figures for the extreme northern counties, emphasising the supplementary nature of the poor law in Scotland.

The data and their implications will be discussed at greater length when the 1818 and 1839 Reports are compared. At this stage it will be sufficient to state that the 1818 Report's major conclusion that assessments caused the number of paupers and the expenditure on them to increase is not substantiated by the evidence. It appears that the conclusion was pre-conceived in fear of a growing trend, and there was concern that payments were too liberal, making it necessary to return to the 'established and sound' principles of the legislation.

A similar movement was occurring in England. Statements in the Select Committees' *Report* demonstrate that certain elements there admired the Scottish system and wanted its adoption. The English Committee concluded that assessments

> have been highly prejudicial to the moral habits, and consequent happiness, of a great body of the people, who have been reduced to the degradation of a dependence upon parochial support; while the rest of the community, including the most industrious class, has been oppressed by a weight of contribution taken from those very means which would otherwise have been applied more beneficially to the supply of employment.[13]

This statement was in print before the Scottish study was undertaken. The English Report concludes that England should restore the system as used in Scotland, "where the local management and maintenance of the Poor has been best conducted". Was the Scottish Report designed to uphold these conclusions and demonstrate to the Scots the perils in deviating from a strict interpretation of the poor law? If so, it would appear that the more generous minded Scots lost the argument, for the rolls and expenditure were substantially lowered after 1818. This reduction, ironically, came at a time of severe unemployment and epidemics. The prevailing philosophy was more closely followed for the next twenty years, the 1818 General Assembly Report in part producing the desired effects, though opening the debate on the merits of the Scottish poor law.

B. *The 1824 Bill and its Rejection*

On 6th April, 1824, Mr Thomas Kennedy of Dunure, a Scottish M.P., introduced into the House of Commons proposed legislation entitled the 'Poor in Scotland Relief Bill'. Mr Kennedy stated that he wished to create uniformity within the system and to revive a spirit of independence among the poor by abolishing legal assessments and introducing a compulsory reliance on voluntary funds, thus forcing parishes to adopt the parochial system and allowing Scotland to enjoy all the benefits of possessing an ideal mode of providing relief. Under the provisions of the Bill the ministers and elders were vested with the administration of all funds arising from church collections and other sources except assessments; the ministers and heritors were to administer the funds arising from an assessment, which could be used only for the support of existing paupers; hence, eventually, voluntary collections would be the sole source of funds. There was no right of appeal, all decisions of the kirk session being final.[14]

This was Mr Kennedy's second attempt to reform the Scottish poor law, the first occurring in 1819 and designed to accomplish the same objectives.[15] There was a great deal of behind-the-scenes activity to determine the best time and means of introducing the 1824 Bill, its backers apparently wishing to sneak it through parliament, but at the same time realising the impossibility of such an attempt. Rev. Dr. Thomas Chalmers of Glasgow was persuaded to write another series of articles expounding the benefit of the measures included in the Bill, without referring to it directly. Chalmers, however, feared the opposition of the larger towns, particularly Edinburgh, Glasgow and Greenock, and of the clergy in the border parishes, where he expected "... a shout of most vehement clamour and opposition" if each parish was not allowed to decide whether to continue the use of a

legal assessment.[16] Cockburn stated that "... if the pauper had no
right to compel relief to be given, the progress of knowledge would
be allowed to operate, and might drive them out of the land",
therefore, let us "... conceal the apparent hardship of denying
redress to the pauper *alone* by letting *nobody* appeal".[17] The Earl of
Minto also felt that the only means of abating pauperism would be to
eliminate assessments.[18]

After the introduction of the Bill opposition against it swelled.
At a meeting on 25th April, the Presbytery of Edinburgh decided to
send petitions denouncing the Bill to both houses. Cockburn wrote
to Kennedy on 7th May that "... the whole fools in the kingdom are
up against the Poor Bill".[19] The following were extracts from the
debate in the Commons:

> Lord A. Hamilton said, that with respect to the measure
> being a boon to the poor of Scotland, he could only
> observe, that the poor of Scotland themselves thought
> it a great grievance. The bill proposed by the Hon.
> member was considered by all who had paid any attention
> to the interests of the poor, and who were in the
> habit of administering to their wants, to be most
> objectionable in principle.

> The Lord Advocate said, that the proposed measure had
> never received the slightest encouragement from any
> public body in Scotland; on the contrary, they all
> concurred in reprobating it. He strongly recommended
> the Hon. member to pause before he again brought it
> forward.

> Mr W. Dundas observed, that the poor of Scotland
> might be left wholly without resource if the system
> of assessments were abolished.[20]

An example of opposition from public bodies comes from the
managers of the St. Cuthbert's Charity Workhouse in Edinburgh, urging
that the provisions of the Bill were "totally inapplicable to the
situation of the Parish, and incapable of being carried into effect
without doing the most essential injury to the interests of the poor".
In particular the managers objected to the removal of the right to
appeal to the Court of Session against kirk session decisions. By
removing the right to assess the parish, it would be impossible

comfortably to relieve the poor. In St. Cuthbert's only one-seventh
of the necessary funds arose from voluntary sources, thus if the
parish was forced to rely solely on them, the poor would be forced
either to beg or to be thrown entirely on the general and casual
charity of the public. Finally, they stated that since the
imposition of a legal assessment, the poor had never claimed relief
as a legal right, nor had those assessed complained that the amount
levied was oppressive in amount.[21] Not only was there such
hostility to the Bill, but it was worth noting Chalmers' ambivalent
attitude which may have ensured the Bill's failure. After a speech
before the General Assembly of the Church of Scotland in which
Chalmers upheld the principles in the Bill, he seconded a motion
that the Assembly should oppose its passage on the grounds that its
clauses were compulsory rather than permissive.[22]

But since the general philosophy of Scotland upheld the merits
of the parochial system, why was the opposition to Kennedy's Bill so
widespread and adamant? The landowners were opposed to any legislation which interfered with a natural social bond. They preferred the
plurality and flexibility of a paternal administration which enabled
them to meet the challenges of changing circumstances. The Kennedy
Bill proposed a set of mechanistic rules and eliminated an element
of choice. The administrators of relief in urban areas were opposed
to the Bill on practical grounds: being responsible for relief on a
daily basis, they were acutely aware of the problem of allocating
resources: they were responsible for distributing the limited funds
to the multitude of applicants, and realised that their available
funds would decrease if assessments could no longer be imposed. Thus,
they would be in a helpless position in the face of even greater
human misery. Chalmers objected to the Bill on the grounds that he
was against any legislation forcing the parishes to adopt a certain
method, so that a parish could no longer choose its methods of

in an attempt at consistency, only the head of the household was counted when possible, otherwise both were included. It was possible to determine the true facts in only sixty-six per cent of the parishes, hence the percentage of the population who were paupers in 1839 is probably overstated relative to 1818. Second, concerning the question of population, for the 1818 Report the 1811 Census was used, as it represented nearly the mid-point in the ten years' data contained in the Report. The 1839 Report used the 1831 Census for its calculations, because the information in the Report was for an average of 1835-36-37, however, it seemed more reasonable to use the 1841 Census. In most cases this tends to make the computed values lower than those in the Report. Third, in the 1818 Report the data under 'Total Funds' show the amounts available for distribution, not the actual amounts distributed, therefore, overstating the expenditure for 1818. Fourth, as portions of twenty-four parishes are in more than one county, and as it would be impossible to determine the proportion of expenditure and number of paupers to allocate to each respective county, the values for these parishes were included in both counties, producing a minimal effect on the results. Fifth, it was assumed that the information contained in the Reports was correct. Finally, in both Reports the percentage of parishes not making returns was not significant.

In order to make meaningful comparisons with the available information, the following calculations were made. average relief per pauper, average relief per head of population, and the percentage of the population receiving relief. These calculations were made on a parish and a county basis; those for the counties are summarised in Table VII. The percentage of parishes assessed in each county in 1818 and 1839 are also given in the Table. As can be seen, 14.5 per cent of the parishes in Scotland were assessed in 1818 and 20.2 per cent in 1839. The figures given here were arrived at by

counting the number of assessed parishes presented in the Reports.
Few of the parishes in northern and western Scotland and the North-
east Lowlands had assessments. The assessed parishes were equally
distributed among the remainder of Scotland, disproving as stated in
the 1839 Report that the bulk of assessed parishes was located along
the English border. Both Reports state that assessments tend to
increase the number of paupers. The 1839 Report gives the percentage
of the whole poor to the population in the unassessed parishes as 3.53,
in those voluntarily assessed it was 3.03, in those legally assessed
it was 3.44, and for the whole country it was 3.42.[24] As these
figures do not support their conclusion, they proceed by stating
"When assessments have long and generally prevailed, however, the
proportion of the poor to the population differs from the above".
They then present data which show that the percentage of the
population who are paupers was greater in the parishes along the
English border. The calculations, on a county basis, using their
data, do not support this conclusion. Table VII illustrates that
the poor, as a percentage of the population, were greater in the
Highland areas, where there was no assessment. Nonetheless, it must
be pointed out that the increase in the ratio of the poor to the
population between 1818 and 1839 was greatest in the Southern
Uplands. If we examine this increase in terms of the northern areas
and the rest of Scotland (which is, of course, the real issue as
these were the assessed as opposed to the unassessed parishes), we
find that the increase in the Lowland areas was nearly twice that of
the northern areas. On the other hand, of the parishes which adopted
a legal assessment between 1818 and 1839, the percentage of parishes
where there was an increase in the poor as a percentage of the
population was 67.3, as compared to an increase for all of Scotland
of 71.3 per cent. Hence, it can be concluded that the increase in
the poor as a percentage of the population cannot be attributed

solely to the imposition of a legal assessment.

The 1839 Report states that with assessments the expenditure per
pauper increase. True, expenditure per head was greater in assessed
parishes, but if the individuals writing the Report had compared the
expenditure per pauper in 1818 with that of 1839, they would have
discovered that such expenditure was in fact decreasing for the whole
of Scotland! Of the parishes undertaking assessments between 1818
and 1839, total expenditure increased in 92.4 per cent and expenditure
per pauper decreased in 48.1 per cent. Admittedly, the latter figure
is a lower per cent than the average figure for all of Scotland (63.8
per cent). The corresponding value for the northern areas is about
60.1 per cent and for the rest of Scotland is about 70.2 per cent.
Thus, for the parishes establishing an assessment for the first time
between 1818 and 1839, the decrease in expenditure per pauper is less
than the national average, lending support to the Report's conclusion.
This is negated in part, however, by the fact that the decrease of
expenditure per pauper was greater in the assessed areas as compared
with the non-assessed. Furthermore, the decrease for the three
counties along the English border was 80.5 per cent. This information
indicates that the parishes were responding to changing economic
conditions, such as a lowering in the price level, with the
response of the assessed parishes more closely correlated to the
needs of their paupers.

Why, if the same data were used, do the conclusions of this
book differ from those of the two Reports? It seems likely that
the 1839 Report was undertaken as an attempt to quell a growing
opposition to low relief payments. The physicians of the period,
particularly Alison, Buchanan, and C. R. Baird, were claiming that
fever epidemics were made worse by the destitute state of the
population: the only way to rid the country of serious epidemics
would be to eliminate destitution. Statements that men cannot

live by the Bible alone, but require food, became more numerous and frequent -- the amount of relief had to be increased! The attack was renewed and strengthened with the epidemic of 1836-38. Alison wrote in 1840,

> ... that the higher ranks in Scotland do much less (and what they do, less systematically, and therefore less effectually) for the relief of poverty and sufferings resulting from it, than those of any other country of Europe which is really well regulated: and much less than experience shows to be necessary in any long inhabited and fully peopled country, in order that the lower ranks may be maintained in tolerable comfort, and a proper foundation laid for their religious and moral improvement.[25]

Such remarks even twenty years earlier would have not been made; the dichotomy between Chalmers and Alison was real and reflected a new sense of moral consciousness.

D. The Medical Profession

The first, and indeed the only, massive attack upon the Scottish poor law system was led by the doctors, and occurred after the English Report of 1834, which praised the Scottish system. The physicians' arguments were clear and concise, strengthened by a wealth of data concerning the out break of epidemic fever. The equation of poverty with moral failure was a sterile starting point: instead, thought about a cure should begin with basic physiological needs.

Dr W. P. Alison[26] of Edinburgh was responsible for initiating the attack, publishing a series of pamphlets in 1840. Earlier criticisms in 1830 by Dr Andrew Buchanan of Glasgow resulted in him losing the post as editor of the *Glasgow Medical Journal*. He later explained that because of his article 'the door was closed against me to all public medical appointments, which younger men were passed over my head to fill'.[27] Dr Buchanan based his comments in 1830 on observations made in an area of Glasgow bounded by the Trongate, Bridgegate, Stockwell, and King Streets. He described the grossly overcrowded and filthy housing conditions and the ill-clothed state of

the inhabitants. The diet and state of the people, he felt, required

the provision of better food, and argued that this need was critical,

as many of the poor died of starvation. He fulminated against the

Corn Laws: 'The people *are starving*, and there is a Law *against the*

importation of FOOD.[28] The immediate and only effect of his

criticisms was the reorganisation of the Medical Department of the

Glasgow Town's Hospital to facilitate the dispensing of medical relief.

By 1840, Dr. Alison was writing after the severe fever epidemics

of 1832-34, 1835-37, and 1838-39. From his personal observations and

those of others in the medical profession he reasoned that the

epidemics were most concentrated in those areas of extreme destitution,

areas where the amounts of poor relief were minimal or non-existent.

He presented data indicating a strong correlation between years of

bad harvests and high unemployment and epidemic years of fever.[29] To

support his argument, Alison gave the following table showing the

proportion of deaths from fever to the whole mortality for selected

British urban areas in 1838:[30]

London	7.7%
Manchester	7.7%
Liverpool	6.9%
Birmingham	5.0%
Leeds	3.6%
Glasgow (1837)	20.4%

It should be noted that there was a typhus epidemic in Glasgow in

1837, nonetheless, he concluded that

> The prevalence of epidemic diseases depends on various
> causes, but the most influential of all is poverty
> and destitution. In every one of the epidemic fevers
> which have ravaged Glasgow, the progress has been slow,
> unless extreme destitution has existed.[31]

Not content with his own observations, Alison circulated a set of

queries to his colleagues in Edinburgh. Generally, the responses

indicated a deplorable state of destitution: unemployed persons

were forced to pawn their furniture and clothes in order to obtain

food and shelter; they could receive assistance, even from private
charities, only after their own resources were exhausted; help was
forthcoming only after the people were sick and in an extreme state
of poverty. To one query Drs. Peterson and Wood responded 'That they
had visited many whose disease might strictly be termed 'want of
proper support'".[32] Mr Wilson stated that destitution was due to
circumstances over which the people had no ccntrol, such as want of
employment, old age, infirmity, widows with young children and wives
deserted by their husbands. The Rev. Dr. Lee, Minister of the Old
Church, described the situation of a mother with five daughters.
They were living in a house with another woman, there were no tables,
chairs, beds, blankets, or cooking utensils. Ironically, this
woman was receiving the highest allowance given by the Edinburgh
Charity Workhouse, 2s. 6d. a week.[33]

Alison argued that relief payments were kept low because the
persons responsible for the administration were also those upon whom
any levy would fall, demonstrating the dichotomy between the kirk
session and the heritors. The kirk session was viewed as the liberal,
kind-hearted element of administration, checked by the stinginess
of the heritors who essentially controlled the purse strings.
Furthermore, the only recourse a pauper had in attempting to increase
his allowance was to appeal to the Court of Session, which was not
easily within his reach. Alison felt the only way to ccrrect the
situation was to subject the decisions of the heritors and kirk
session to an easily accessible local court.

He also criticised the practice of granting relief on the basis
of moral character. By excluding sinners from the assistance of
public relief, the innocent often were the ones to suffer.

> ... we punish children along with parents; we punish
> in many instances neighbours and acquaintances among
> the poor themselves, who supply, in a certain degree,
> from their own scanty resources, the deficiency of other
> charity; and in many instances we punish a much larger

> number of the public, to whom such sufferers, rather than
> starve in silence, will make their wants known in some
> way or other, and who have not the means of granting
> relief with the same discrimination as public charities.[34]

The moral elements of the applicants should serve only as a guide to
the kind of relief to be granted.

Alison desired that provision be made for a general uniform legal
assessment, with the amounts considerably increased. This practice
would be more just for both the higher and lower orders. The higher
would benefit as all its members would be forced to contribute their
full share, rather than some shouldering the burdens of others. The
lower orders would benefit as the amounts would be more easily
adapted to their real needs. Moreover, he felt that relief received
from a legal fund would not be as degrading as relief from private
charity; the former would be a secure amount, whereas the latter
depends upon the whims of the giver. Furthermore, the unemployed
also should be given assistance. Indigence should be the only
requirement for relief.

As a result of Alison's endeavours, in 1840 an association was
formed in Edinburgh for the purpose of obtaining an inquiry into
pauperism in Scotland. Its 64 members included influential landowners,
merchants, ministers, professors, physicians, and advocates. At their
first meeting they unanimously adopted several resolutions. First,
there were reasons for believing that the poor in parts of Scotland
were subject to a greater degree of want and misery than those in
England and most other civilised countries. Second, the miserable
conditions of the poor in Edinburgh were attributable mainly to the
inadequacy of the sum legally raised for their support, to the influx
of poor from other parishes without a legal assessment, and to the
ravages of disease. Third, the peace and well-being of all ranks of
society were affected by the conditions of the poor. Fourth, it was
the obligation of Christian benevolence that the provision to the

poor should raise them permanently above the moral degradation and
vice to which they were so readily exposed. Fifth, as the existing
state in Scotland could not have arisen without defects in either
the system of administration or the poor law, an official commission
should be established to determine the defects and propose remedies.[35]
By 1842 the town councils of thirteen of the principal towns in
Scotland had petitioned the government requesting an official
inquiry. The tide had turned.

By 1840 the work of Alison was gaining success because events
affected not only the poor, but also the middle classes. All classes
suffered by the fever epidemics of the 1830's, resulting in the middle
classes feeling endangered and, hence, arguing for programs designed
to eliminate the threat of fever. Therefore, the poor benefited as
a result of the correlation Alison made between indigence and the
spread of fever. Furthermore, as will be seen, the middle classes
also faced a financial threat, the immediate one being a lack of
church accommodation, especially in urban areas. This restricted
church door collections, necessitating either a voluntary or legal
assessment with the middle classes bearing the major share. These
factors were the primary ones causing a change of attitude in the
late 1830's toward the Scottish poor law. These attitudes are,
indeed, reflected in the petitions sent to the government requesting
an official inquiry.

E. *Discontent of the Lower Classes*

Working class protests against the poor law in Scotland were
centred around the Glasgow-Paisley industrial area. Furthermore,
such protests were made only when there was large scale unemployment
among the operatives, particularly the handloom weavers, and were
concerned with providing such men with assistance from the public
funds. Apparently the Radical movement of 1815-22 did not champion

the cause of the destitute.[36] The Scottish Chartist, unlike their English brethren, did not take issue with Scottish poor relief administration, other than to oppose the 1845 Poor Law Amendment Act (Scotland).[37] This is particularly ironic, since Paisley was a stronghold for the Chartist movement, and the Reverend Patrick Brewster, minister of Paisley Abbey was a leader.

In a petition to the Govan kirk session in 1816, twelve unemployed handloom weavers requested relief from the poor's fund. All the petitioners testified that their wages had decreased between one-half and two-thirds of the former level, with the hours of work being about twelve per day. The kirk session agreed to give each two pecks of meal until the heritors could be consulted, who decided that the petitioners could not be relieved from the poor's fund, but that a subscription should be undertaken on their behalf. Finally, in an act of humanity the heritors stated they

> sincerely regret and strongly condemn the total want
> of economy, when trade was good, which appears in
> the declarations of some of the petitioners; and,
> on this occasion, deem it their duty warmly to
> recommend industry, good management, and careful
> economy, to the operative classes in this parish,
> for the time to come.[38]

In 1819 about 150 men went through the streets of Bridgeton, Glasgow, carrying a sign proclaiming "public begging for want of work". One or two of their number went into every shop, while the others remained outside. As a result of this action, a large soup kitchen was established. Its funds were "precariously supplied by voluntary contribution".[39]

The troubles of the handloom weavers in Paisley brought forth a flood of petitions in 1839. They were clearly written by well-educated individuals thoroughly versed in the law, possibly one being the rebel minister Patrick Brewster, a champion for the poor; he represented the weavers' cause before the session and heritors. Apparently the overseers for the poor in Paisley and the kirk session

132.

had agreed to aid all destitute children under fourteen years of age and the old and infirm. The heritors felt that this action should be postponed until a committee could study the situation, effectively ending the issue. Rift within the Paisley administration was further widened in 1841, when another petition was presented to the session and heritors. Brewster again represented their cause, referring to a resolution passed on 2nd July, 1841, that the overseers should ensure that no case of starvation occurred in the parish. Hence, Brewster moved that the petitioners should be relieved under the terms of the resolution. At this point the Rev. Mr Burns moved an adjournment, which was seconded by Mr Wilson of Deanside. Without taking a vote most of the members left the meeting. Those remaining seized the opportunity and approved Brewster's motion. Their efforts, however, were in vain. The heritors declared the meeting illegal.[40]

Brewster was perhaps the most outspoken of the Established Church's ministers against the administration of the Scottish poor law. He argued that "... the administration of the Poor Law in Scotland has entirely failed to accomplish its object, and that great evil has resulted to the country, and much suffering to the poor, from unrelieved destitution". Continuing on, he argued that unemployment caused by economic depression was not the fault of the labourer, hence justice demands from the wealthy an adequate and ample relief for the disabled and unemployed poor.[41]

Events in Paisley may have had some impact upon Westminster, causing eventually another inquiry into the poor of Scotland in 1844. On 16th December, 1840 the managers of the Paisley Workhouse passed the following motion:

> That this Board do Petition Her Majesty Government to
> extend the investigation now going on as to the sanatory
> conditions of the labouring classes in Scotland, so as
> to include the condition generally of the poor in
> Scotland particularly in cities and large towns with

a view to an early and complete alteration of the
existing Poor Laws.

This was followed by another memorial in 1841, which stated in part -

That your memorialists are firmly persuaded that the
parochial and voluntary assistance rendered to the
poor particularly in large towns and in many of the
parishes in the Highlands and Islands of Scotland is
altogether inadequate to procure for them the
necessary supply of food, clothing, and lodging,
in consequence of which the poor have suffered
severely from disease; and in those parts of the
country where no assessment is raised the condition
of the poor is deplorable.[42]

F. *Secession from the Established Church, 1740-1843*

The fatal blow to the old Scottish poor law was dealt by the

Disruption of 1843. As the Established Church was responsible by law

for administering poor relief, any secession movement which fragmented

its strength put to the hazard the pitifully small sums available for

poor relief. The general decrease in church door collections during

the period under consideration can be accounted for by two factors.

First, the period witnessed a substantial increase in absentee land-

lords. Second, there was secession from the Established Church and

the shift of members to dissenting places of worship. The effect of

these factors was to create a situation where the poor's funds were

insufficient to meet emergencies.

The cause of the first secession from the Church was the

restoration in 1712 of patronage in appointing the clergy. Patronage

was not forced upon the parishes until the General Assembly Act of

1732, which stated that only the heritors and kirk session could

choose the minister. Ebenezer Erskine, minister at Stirling, led

a group which argued that a minister should not be forced upon the

congregation. After a period of compromises the General Assembly

of 1740 voted to depose eight ministers. These men were responsible

for the formation of the Burghers. The result of the Secession was

that the kirk session funds were unable to meet unusual emergencies.

The numbers in the Established Church were further reduced by the Second Secession in 1761. It was led by Thomas Gillespie and was also a result of opposition to patronage. This group founded the Relief Church. The problem, however, did not become critical until the Disruption of 1843. Again, the dispute centred primarily around the question of patronage. The split resulted in approximately two-fifths of the clergy leaving the Establishment and forming the Free Church, which, under the leadership of Chalmers carried out a massive building programme and became a strong, viable competitor to the Establishment.

Besides decreasing church collections, secession had another important effect upon the operation of the poor law. The dissenting congregations had no legal restrictions placed upon their funds, whereas the Established Church was required to spend one-half of its collections on poor relief. As the kirk sessions could not discriminate on a religious basis in the granting of relief, many elders argued that an unfair burden was placed upon the members of the Church, particularly if there was no legal assessment. Hence only a small percentage of the population were contributing towards the support of the poor. Under these circumstances, it is not surprising that the Church, through its representatives, the ministers, demanded a change in the administrative framework with respect to poor relief.

Even before the Disruption of 1843, it was evident that the Church wished to divest itself of its administrative duties. The General Assembly of 1841 passed a resolution stating it was their belief that statements concerning the destitution and sufferings of large portions of the population were all too true. And as long as the heritors refused to construct new churches and pay the ministers' stipends from the tithe administered by them, these expenses would

have to be made from the church collections, decreasing the amount
available for poor relief. Hence, it was proposed that the government
make an official inquiry into the subject.[43] This action came only
two years after the publication of their Report of 1839 - a Report
expressing favourable opinions towards the Scottish system of poor
relief. The memorial, however, did stress that the Church believed
that the "two great principles of the Scottish system of poor relief"
should be maintained: legal allowances should only be supplementary
to assistance from private charity, and relief should not be granted
to the able-bodied unemployed.[44]

G. *Conclusions*

The Scottish poor laws were rarely questioned prior to 1815,
because the intensity of destitution had never been sufficient to
place pressure on their operation. The war years, 1795-1815,
increased the expenditure on the poor, as a result of rising prices
and a need to provide for the widows and children of deceased
soldiers. Appeals to patriotism probably prevented any out-cry
against the soaring trend in poor relief expenditure. But the war
years also witnessed the formation of another factor: industrialisation and the resultant urbanisation intensified the magnitude of
destitution to such a degree that it could no longer be ignored.
Ironically, parallel events were occurring south of the border, the
outcome, however, yielding different results· the English eventually
tightened their poor laws, the Scots ostensibly liberalising theirs.

The 1818 and 1839 Reports were Church inspired attempts to
demonstrate the evils of a system of legal assessments. These
backward looking, whitewash Reports, especially that of 1818, also
received English guidance and encouragement, as conclusions upholding
the Scottish poor relief philosophy would lend substantial weight to
those in England fighting the 'allowance-in-aid-of-wages' system.

Kennedy's 1824 Bill, indeed, was an attempt to ensure the perpetuation in Scotland of the sacred principles of the parochial system of relief. Its defeat placed its backers in a defensive position from which they were never able to recover.

The working class movements to obtain public relief in times of unemployment could not dissolve the apathy of the middle classes, who failed to realise that unemployment was not the fault of the workers. The teachings of Brewster caught the imaginations of only a few men. The security of the middle class was not sufficiently jeopardised.

The only effective opposition to the poor laws came from the doctors, ironically gaining support from the epidemics which failed to make class distinctions. The doctors began their reasonings at the nether end of society where the ills of deprivation were most concentrated; the moralists of the poor law couched their case in terms of an irremediable residual. This dichotomising of approach is general in poor law discussion: that between concern with immediate and cumulative degradation among the poorest, and that which sees society as a totality.

The doctors' case would have eventually led to a change in the laws, but the Disruption of 1843 effectively sealed the fate of the old system. It is surely significant that Chalmers was instrumental in achieving the destruction of the old parochial system which he so much admired and of which his famous St. John's experiment was a vivid example. The majority of the middle class did not leave the Establishment, so solely with them was placed the burden of financing the system of relief in those parishes without a legal assessment. They were unwilling to meet this responsibility. Indeed, it was only when the middle class felt the direct effects of epidemics and increased financial burdens that movements to change the old Scottish poor law were successful.

137.

1. Anon, *Glasgow Polity*, 1785, p. 1.

2. Anon, *Glasgow Polity*, 1785, pp. 27-8.

3. Anon, *A Letter on Poor Rates*, 1807, pp. 26-7.

4. 1818 Report, p. 22.

5. Mark Blaug, "Myth of Old Poor Law", in *JEH*, 1963, p. 159.

6. Mark Blaug, "Poor Law Report Re-examined", in *JEH*, 1964, p. 229.

7. 1818 Report, p. 25.

8. 1818 Report, p. 29.

9. 1818 Report, p. 30.

10. 1818 Report, p. 31.

11. 1818 Report, p. 33.

12. See Chapter 2.

13. *Report from Select Committee on the Poor Laws*, 1818, p. 4.

14. T. C. Hansard, *Parliamentary Debates*, vol. II, New Series, p. 226.

15. Hansard, *Parliamentary Debates*, vol. 39, pp. 1469-1476.

16. Cockburn, *Letters*, pp. 94-6.

17. Cockburn, *Letters*, p. 30.

18. Cockburn, *Letters*, pp. 100-1.

19. *Caledonian Mercury*, 25 April, 1824.

20. Cockburn, *Letters*, p. 118.

21. St. Cuthbert's Charity Workhouse Minutes, 11th May, 1824.

22. Cockburn, *Letters*, p. 120.

23. The following men were on the Committee: Alexander Dunlop (solicitor, Edinburgh), Rev. William Muir (St. Stephen's, Edinburgh), Rev. Alexander Brunton (The Tron, Edinburgh), Rev. David Dickson (St. Cuthbert's, Collegiate charge, Edinburgh), Rev. Robert Gordon (St. Giles, Edinburgh), Rev. Patrick Clason (Buccleuch, Edinburgh), Rev. A. L. Simpson (Kirknewton, Edinburgh), Rev. John Hunter (The Tron, second charge, Edinburgh), Rev. John Paul (St Cuthbert's, Edinburgh), Rev. William Cunningham (Trinity, Edinburgh), Rev. James Grant (S. Leith, Edinburgh), Rev. Thomas Guthrie (Old Greyfriars, Edinburgh), Sir James W. Moncrieff (judge, Edinburgh), Sir Charles D. Fergusson (5th baronet, Kilkerran, Ayrshire), Sir James Forrest (Bart., Colinton, Mid-Lothian), David Monypenny (solicitor, St. Andrews), Robert Bell, John C. Swinton (solicitor, Dunse, Berwick), and John Shaw Stewart.

138.

24. 1839 Report, p. 18.

25. Alison, *Observations*, p. viii.

26. W. P. Alison was born in 1790 near Edinburgh, the son of a minister. In 1815 he became one of the first medical officers of the Edinburgh New Town Dispensary, a medical charity supported by private subscription. During his first 18 months at the Dispensary, he was an advocate of home visitation of the sick poor; over one-quarter of his 8062 patients during this period were attended to in their homes. At this time of his life he made the connection between destitution and fever, publishing a series of quarterly reports in the *Edinburgh Medical and Surgical Journal*. In 1819 he was appointed to the chair of Medical Jurisprudence at Edinburgh University. Shortly thereafter he was appointed to the chair of Institute of Medicine (Physiology) and then to the chair of Medicine. In the cholera epidemic of 1831-2 he represented the College of Physicians on the Board of Health, leading the struggle to remove patients to houses of refuge. Beginning in 1840 he entered into a series of written debates with Dr Thomas Chalmers, then professor of Divinity at Edinburgh on the condition of and remedies for the poor. In his report in 1842 on sanitary conditions in Edinburgh, Alison took to task Chadwick for his views on the causes of poverty. He stated that the 1845 Act was "framed with studious conservatism". His public activities ended with his first epileptic attack suffered in 1846. See W. T. Gairdner, *Physician and Naturalist*, Glasgow, 1889, pp. 388-425 and J. H. F. Brotherston, "William Pultney Alison, Scottish Pioneer of Social Medicine", in *The Medical Officer*, 6 June 1958, pp. 331-336. Professor Flinn has stated that Dr Alison occupied "... a similar position in Scotland in relation to poor law and public health reform to that held by Chadwick in England". See *Report on Sanitary Conditions*, M. W. Flinn, ed., p. 23.

27. *Memoirs and Portraits of One Hundred Glasgow Men*, 1886, p. 45.

28. A. Buchanan, "Report of the Diseases which prevailed among the poor of Glasgow, during the summer of 1830", in *Glasgow Medical Journal*, 1830, vol. 3, p. 447.

29. Alison, *Observations*, pp. 12-3.

30. Alison, "Further Illustrations", pp. 305-6.

31. Alison, "Further Illustrations", p. 309.

32. Alison, "Illustrations", p. 220.

33. Alison, *Observations*, pp. 11-12.

34. Alison, *Observations*, pp. 140-41.

35. *Report of the Association for Obtaining Inquiry into Pauperism in Scotland*, pp. 1-2.

36. William Roach, 1970.

37. Leslie Wright, 1953, and Alexander Wilson, 1970.

38. Govan Heritors Records, 28th July, 1819.

39. *Glasgow Chronicle*, 7th December, 1819.

40. Abbey Kirk Session Minutes, 5th January, 1843.

41. Patrick Brewster, p. 86 and p. 97.

42. Paisley Workhouse Minutes, 17th February, 1841.

43. *Proceedings of the General Assembly*, pp. 324-25.

44. *Proceedings of the General Assembly*, p. 44.

CHAPTER 8: THE 1844 REPORT AND THE POOR LAW

AMENDMENT ACT (SCOTLAND)

The growing discontent with the operation of the Scottish poor law was not seriously lessened by the 1839 Report, which raised more questions than it answered. The Disruption in 1843 precipitated the final crisis, for, because of the drastic fall in church door collections, the Established Church felt it could not continue supplying all the parish poor under the voluntary system. Accordingly, a special commission was appointed in 1844 to make a thorough inquiry into the operation of the poor law in Scotland and to make recommendations on ways of changing that system in order to eliminate existing defects.

The following men were appointed to the Committee: Robert Viscount Melville,[1] Robert Montgomerie (8th Lord Belhaven), Henry Home Drummond,[2] James Campbell of Craigie (Ayr, Ayrshire), Edward Twisleton,[3] Patrick Macfarlan,[4] and James Robertson (Minister of Ellon, Aberdeenshire). Besides sending questionnaires to all the parishes, at least two members personally visited and examined every presbytery. These visits were beneficial, as the answers received from the questionnaires exhibited considerable misunderstanding of the questions. The visits also caused the Committee to stress that the conditions of the poor should be compared with those of the working class, otherwise an exaggerated impression of the poors' discomfort might be received.

In terms of general poor law history the 1844 Scottish Report is significant, when compared with the English Report of 1834; indeed, similar methods were used on both occasions. Nearly one hundred per cent of Scotland's parishes submitted returns, and the evidence given before the Committee and the returns received are contained in seven volumes, nearly 15,000 pages. It produced a comprehensive study of the life and conditions of the poorer classes and a detailed understanding of the operation of the poor law. The picture was one

of abject poverty. The Commissioners were overwhelmed by Scotland's
problem of destitution, and their Report was an attempt to redress the
situation. Even so, they stressed that the legislature should amend
and repair the existing system, rather than introduce a new one,
foreign to the feelings and habits of the country. The Committee
recommended that no changes in the law be made with respect to the
type of individuals eligible for relief: the impotent, old, infirm
and orphaned continued to be regarded as proper objects of public
charity. In general, if need could not be proven, any claim to relief
was strongly resisted in order to avoid the encouragement of vice by
too ready advances made at the public expense. No fault could be
found in this practice.

The Committee also agreed with the prevalent mode of handling
the able-bodied unemployed. Such persons were often given temporary
relief from the funds during periods of sickness; rarely were they
given aid from the poor's fund when unemployed. The following
expresses the Committee's attitude towards relieving the able-bodied:

> While in the case of the able-bodied again, all that
> humanity or even Christian philanthropy requires to be
> done, is that we furnish them with the means of
> developing their own resources. We learn, upon an
> authority which, if rightly understood and applied,
> is no less conclusive in political economy than in
> religion, and the disregard of which in any relation
> of human life, cannot fail to be attended with
> injurious results, that if a man will not work,
> neither should he eat. The over-looking of this
> salutory maxim in the provisions of statutes
> appointed to regulate the administration of
> charitable funds, - a maxim, on the incontrovertible
> equity of which it were more waste of time to insist, -
> has been proved by experience to be productive of
> the most serious evils in the social system.[5]

The Committee believed that beneficial results would be obtained if
workhouses were provided for the relief, under discipline, of the
able-bodied unemployed. They referred to the English Act of 1834,
which established workhouses as a means and character test, indicating
a willingness to conform to the English pattern by using English

legislation as a sanction and control. It was felt that only the
most destitute and deserving would be willing to undergo the rigours
of a workhouse.

Generally, however, the Committee accepted the Scottish tradition
that the able-bodied should never be relieved from the public funds.
If circumstances indicated a need to provide the unemployed with
assistance, the source of funds should be voluntary subscriptions.
The Committee thus recommended no change in the existing practices,
even though they recognised that relief from voluntary subscriptions
was invariably slow in coming, and was given only after severe hardships had been endured. Unemployed labourers frequently were relieved
during periods of severe unemployment by public voluntary subscriptions administered independently of the poor's funds. The Committee
lauded this practice, as

> the operation of the present law makes as near an approach
> as is attainable, under existing circumstances at least,
> to the system of relief which sound principle points out
> as applicable to the case of the able-bodied poor. It
> preserves to the objects relieved their status in society;
> it keeps the family circle with all its invaluable
> relations unbroken; it administers relief through a
> friendly community both an opportunity and the means
> of dispensing their charity, in supplement of its own
> allowances, with judgement and discrimination. Thus,
> while it relieves the wants of the needy, it excites
> in them at the same time emotions of gratitude, makes
> them realize the value of good conduct and character,
> probably opens up to them, if deserving, in case of
> their diminished capabilities and by all these means,
> and others of a like nature, fosters in them through a
> powerful appeal to every better principle the full
> development of a contented, thankful, and independent
> industry.[6]

The Committee recommended that the sole means of preventing mass
unemployment, such as occurred in the handloom weaving industry,
would be to encourage employment of a different nature or in a
different locality. With respect to the Highlands, the Committee
felt that any assistance to the able-bodied would substantially
reduce industry. They argued that the Highland labourer, under the
stimulus of immediate reward, was willing to exert himself in order

to accomplish a given task. When the work was finished, he relapsed
"into his wonted lethargy".

After briefly reviewing the sources of funds for poor relief, the
Committee stated it was their opinion *"That the funds raised for the
relief of the poor, and the provision made for them out of the funds
raised for their relief, is, in many Parishes throughout Scotland,
insufficient".*[7] Nonetheless, the Committee was opposed to a compulsory
assessment, as that still would not ensure an adequate allowance. But
the Committee did not condemn assessments: the necessity of imposing
one depended upon local circumstances. Furthermore, they stated that
the general feeling against assessments was gradually diminishing;
that more parishes would adopt that means of raising funds, and that
no evidence could be found to indicate that the imposition of a legal
assessment reduced church collections.

The Committee recommended that in every parish where an assessment was imposed, the church collections should be left to the sole
disposal of the kirk session in order to provide occasional charity,
that is small payments designed to prevent people coming on the roll.
By leaving the church collections at the disposal of the kirk session
in assessed parishes, the amount of such collections would probably
increase. Moreover, the character and condition of the poor would
be likely to improve if they were not regarded as 'registered' paupers.
These policies were adhered to primarily as a result of the testimony
of Rev. Dr. Gordon, who stated that his influence over the people was
greater when he was able to give some pecuniary assistance.

Although the Committee felt that allowances to paupers were often
inadequate, they decided that it would be detrimental to allow any
outside interference to arise in determining the amount. Only people
familiar with local circumstances could possess adequate information
to establish the allowance. Even though first impressions may indicate
inadequate allowances, closer examination may reveal a different

situation. Furthermore, when determining the amount of assistance to be given, the pauper's character should be taken into account. For these reasons the Commissioners felt that the decision of the parochial managers concerning the amount of the allowance should be final; there should be no right of appeal.

The Report then described how social change could affect the operation of the law. Under the old crofting system the inhabitants of the Highlands were closely connected with one another, each willing to offer whatever help lay in his power to relatives or neighbours who were less fortunate. After the clearances the crofters either migrated or were collected into villages on the coast. As a result, many who were able to help others now found themselves facing great difficulties in obtaining their own livelihood. The clearances also altered the degree of sympathy between the paupers and the occupants of the land.

The Committee deplored that so little medical assistance was available to the poor, and recommended the provision of much more medical relief which was, they judged, a proper charge upon the poor's fund. This policy would be very beneficial, as the susceptibility of contagion is increased greatly whenever the constitution is weakened by destitution, dissipation, or an unhealthy atmosphere. The policy would be easier to implement and the poor better provided for if a poorhouse was established in every parish with a population in excess of 6-8,000. Thus, the Committee argued in favour of establishing a system of poorhouses.

The Committee were highly critical of Scotland's settlement laws. If a pauper could not prove his settlement, all relief was refused him, even though he was in a state of destitution. Furthermore, people were often denied admission to infirmaries because of doubts as to their parish of settlement. The Committee argued that great abuses arose from the pass system; the parishes were sending people

to their claimed parish of settlement without ascertaining precisely
where they belong. In order to correct these wrongs the Committee
recommended that the parish in which a person was found destitute be
required immediately to relieve him, and that such relief should
continue until the parish of settlement was known. The expenses of
interim maintenance, and other expenses, would be recoverable from
the parish ultimately found liable. Only one exception to this
policy should be allowed: English and Irish paupers should be
removed immediately to their respective countries. Implementation
of this policy would bring Scottish legislation in line with English
and Irish legislation.

The Committee felt that the allegation that people flocked to
towns for the purpose of obtaining relief was much exaggerated. They
believed that the poor in rural areas were better provided for than
the poor in the towns. The Committee argued it would be truer to
state that agricultural labourers leave the country for the towns
after they are unable to do heavy work, thus migrating to towns in
search of some form of light employment. Furthermore, it was
difficult for retired farm labourers to procure cottages in their
vicinity, and so were often thus being forced to leave. After making
these observations the Committee recommended that the necessary period
of residence for obtaining a settlement be increased from three to
seven years. The reason for this proposal was that the parish where
an individual spent most of his life enjoyed the benefit of his
labour, hence it should support him in old age. During the seven
years' period the person would be required to maintain himself
without parochial relief or having recourse to common begging.
Furthermore, a settlement by residence could be acquired only by
a native of Scotland.

The only major change in the law which the Committee proposed

was in the area of administration. They recommended that a Board of
Supervision on a national basis, consisting of unpaid members, be
established for a limited period of time. Each parish would submit
semi-annual statements to the Board showing the numbers and condition
of their poor and the amount of relief supplied to each. All
complaints against the local managers were to be made to the Board,
which was to have the fullest power of inquiry and remonstrance. The
Board was to submit annual reports to the Secretary of State on the
condition and management of the poor throughout Scotland. Furthermore, the parochial managers would be required to appoint a salaried
clerk to make the reports to, and to conduct all correspondence with
the Board. The clerk's salary was to be fixed by the local managers.
If a rural parish was not assessed, the management would remain with
the kirk session and heritors. Heritors were redefined to include
all persons who held a valued rent to the amount of at least £5 Scots
(8s. 3d, Sterling). If a rural parish was assessed, or became
assessed at some future date, the management was to be undertaken by
the kirk session, heritors, and a certain number of persons chosen
by the ratepayers who were not heritors. Thus, all persons paying
the assessment would be represented in the management.

For the purposes of poor relief and settlement all parishes
within the parliamentary boundaries of any burgh should be united
and held as one parish. The managers in such a situation would
consist wholly or chiefly of individuals elected by the ratepayers,
plus the provost and chief magistrate, *ex officio*. Each ratepayer
would possess a number of votes in proportion to the amount of
property on which he was assessed.

In the short period of time available to them the Committee
were unable to digest and analyse the large quantity of data
collected from the parochial returns. They based their Report and
recommendations upon the evidence collected in personal testimony.

The Committee was not unanimous; Edward Twisleton presented a
dissenting report. He felt that the Committee had not gone far enough
in its recommendations: equality throughout Scotland could be obtained
only by having a national compulsory assessment, and appeals to the
sheriff courts should be allowed. Furthermore, he felt that the
able-bodied unemployed should be provided with relief in workhouses,
as was the case in England.

Action on the Committee's Report was swift. On 11th February,
1845, Lord Dalmeny asked if a bill was to be introduced to change the
Scottish system of poor relief, as recommended by the late Committee.
Sir James Graham, the Secretary for the Home Department, answered
that the government needed time to consider the matter, as any Act
changing a system which had been in operation for nearly two hundred
years must be undertaken with caution. On 2nd April, 1845, the Lord
Advocate rose to introduce the Bill, which was necessary, he said,
because of the great public pressure to correct the abuses with regard
to the poor of Scotland. Little opposition to the Bill was recorded.
Indeed, only one change was suggested; Mr Edward Ellice argued,
without success, that a compulsory assessment was needed and should
be levied by people other than local authorities. On 12th June, 1845,
the Bill received its second reading.

The Act's provisions were similar to the recommendations of the
1844 Committee, and the law as it existed before 1845 was not materially
changed. Indeed, the Act only provided machinery for the administration
of relief to the poor; no change was made in the description of persons
legally entitled to relief. The most significant provisions were two:
the establishment of a national Board of Supervision, and the provision
that if an assessment was in the future imposed, it had to be laid
annually thereafter.

The Board of Supervision was the first central poor law authority
in Scotland. Its nine members met twice yearly on the first Wednesday

of February and August; all gave their services gratuitously except
one, who was paid to carry on the daily duties of the Board. The
following were the nine members: the Lord Provosts of Edinburgh and
Glasgow, the Solicitor-General, the Sheriffs-Depute of Perth, Renfrew,
Ross and Cromarty, and three others nominated by the Crown. The
Board was empowered to inquire into the management of the poor in
every parish and burgh in Scotland and to conduct any special
inquiries it might think necessary. If a pauper felt that his
pension was inadequate, he could appeal to the Board of Supervision,
a provision going beyond the recommendation of the Commissioners.

In every parish and burgh the administration of relief was
vested in a group of men called the Parochial Board, their composition
depending upon local circumstances. In all unassessed rural parishes
the kirk sessions and heritors were to continue with the administration of the law. If an assessment was imposed, the Parochial Board
was to consist of a fixed number of heritors, a fixed number from
the kirk session, and a fixed number elected at large by the ratepayers. In each case the number chosen was to be determined at the
local level, every arrangement being subject to the approval of the
Board of Supervision. For the purposes of providing relief, rural
parishes were permitted to combine. Moreover, if the population of
a parish or combined parishes exceeded 5,000, a poorhouse could be
erected. In combined parishes and in all burghs the Parochial
Board was to consist of not more than thirty members elected by the
ratepayers, four chosen by the magistrates, and four chosen by the
kirk session. All elected officials served for one year and were
eligible for re-election.

The Parochial Boards were required to meet on the first
Tuesday of February and August. They were to compile a list of the
poor and appoint a paid inspector of the poor, who was to keep all
the records concerning poor relief, and to visit the poor in their

homes at least twice a year. The Boards were empowered to raise funds
by assessment, but, once imposed an assessment became an annual levy,
unless the Board of Supervision agreed to a change. Furthermore, funds
raised by assessment were applicable to the relief of occasional poor.
If an assessment was imposed, the church collections were to be at
the sole disposal of the kirk session.

In assessed parishes the Boards were to fix the amount of the
assessment annually and to make a list of those liable to it. One of
the following three modes of assessment had to be specified with the
initial imposition: (a) one-half on owners and one-half on the
occupiers and tenants of lands and heritages within the parish, the
rate laid according to the annual value of rent; (b) one-half on
owners according to the annual value of rent and one-half on the
whole inhabitants according to their means and substance; (c) equal
percentage on the annual value of lands and heritages within the
parish and on the estimated income of all the inhabitants. If the
second mode was used, means and substances under thirty pounds could
not be assessed.

Several provisions for medical assistance were made. The
Parochial Boards were ordered to supply necessary medical relief to
all paupers, with the expense of such relief to form a proper burden
on the poor's fund. The Boards also were required to provide
clothing and education to those in need of such items. All lunatic
paupers on the rolls were to be placed in asylums.

A number of changes were made with respect to settlement. The
period for acquiring a settlement by residence was increased from
three to five years, and as was previously the case, during this
time the individual could not have recourse to begging or public
charity. Destitute persons were to be relieved, although having no
settlement in the parish to which they applied, and the parish
providing assistance could later recover all expenses from the

parish of settlement. Finally, parishes were empowered to remove to their respective countries all English and Irish paupers who had not acquired a settlement in Scotland.

The effect of the Act was immediate. Increases in the number of poor, in total expenditure, and in the number of parishes levying a legal assessment took place within the year. Out of 878 parishes in 1842-3, 230 had a legal assessment; by 1845-6 the number had increased to 448, of which 379 used annual value of rent as the mode of taxation. Total expenditure on the poor for the year ended 1st February, 1845 was £258,814 19s. 11d., and for 1st February, 1846 was £295,232 8s. 1d. The number of poor on the rolls for the two periods was 63,070 and 69,432, respectively. The number of parishes levied increased much more than did expenditure on the poor.

Change in the Scottish poor law came eleven years after changes in England. The English Act of 1834, however, represented a major shift in philosophy; this was not the case for the Scottish Act of 1845. Despite an apparent encouragement to impose a legal assessment, the establishment of the Board of Supervision, and the granting of medical relief, the basic tenets of Scottish poor relief were upheld. The able-bodied unemployed still were denied assistance from the public funds; only the aged, orphaned, and impotent were regarded as proper objects of charity. Allowances continued to be viewed as supplementary in nature. Little was gained by the poor in Scotland.

---

1. Robert Saunders Dundas (1771-1851), 2nd Viscount; in 1794 was elected M.P. for Hastings; in 1800 chosen as one of the keepers of the signet for Scotland; in 1801 elected M.P. for Midlothian; in 1830 retired from political life and returned to Edinburgh.

2. Elected M.P. for Stirlingshire in 1821 and served until 1831; in 1841 elected M.P. for Perthshire.

3. Was an assistant Poor Law Commissioner in England in 1839; in 1845 chosen Poor Law Commissioner for Ireland.

4. In 1824 replaced Chalmers at St. John's and the following year
    moved to St. Enoch's where he stayed until 1832, when be
    became the minister of the West Kirk at Greenock.

5. 1844 Report, vol. 1, p. xiv.

6. 1844 Report, vol. 1, p. xiviii.

7. 1844 Report, vol. 1, p. xiv.

Conclusions

The starting point for discussion of the treatment of the poor must be the parameters set by the law, for to understand the practices it is necessary to appreciate the framework within which they were designed to operate. The laws clearly established those eligible for relief, the sources of funds, and the administrators. Accordingly, the proper objects of relief were the aged, the orphaned, and the impotent. The fund for the poor consisted of one-half of the church door collections, certain fines and fees, legacies, and, when necessary, the proceeds of a legal assessment. Poor relief in each rural parish was administered by the kirk sessions and heritors and in each burgh by the magistrates and town council. Yet, within this seemingly rigid framework considerable flexibility was present, as each parish determined the criteria for the granting of relief and the amount of the allowance. The decisions by the administrators on these important aspects did not necessarily embody the intent of the legislation, especially as a philosophy of self-reliance and relief only as a supplement to other sources of livelihood became the prevailing guideline in many parishes during the late eighteenth century. This latter element was an attempt to preserve the parochial system during a period of rapid economic and social change: the emergence of a distinctive urban system was a reflection of these changing conditions, whereas the work of Thomas Chalmers was an attempt to reverse the process.

In both the law and practice the Scottish poor law consisted of two sub-systems, the rural and the urban. Each was designed to meet the features peculiar to each setting. Generally, the administrative practice followed in rural parishes between 1745 and 1845 was that the kirk sessions assumed sole responsibility, unless financial difficulties arose and the imposition of a legal assessment became a threat, when the heritors often took emergency action. The kirk sessions, therefore, can be viewed as the more liberal element of administration, wishing to ease the sufferings of the deserving destitute; their desire, however, was held in check by the heritors who had ultimate control over the outlays. In the burghs the magistrates and town councils delegated their authority to elected lay officials and a system of indoor relief evolved, later to be augmented by out-pensions. Both types of administrative units in order to minimise expenditure and to try to recompense the funds developed the idea of relief as a loan. Paupers were 'tied to the box' at the time of enrolment upon the regular funds, being forced to sign dispositions making the poor's fund heir to their belongings.

Under the operation of the parochial system major reliance was placed upon the use of voluntary sources of funds, as it was feared that the poor might demand relief as a *right* if the source of funds was other than voluntary. Furthermore, the paternalistic approach of the parochial system assured that the destitute received charitable assistance in times of need, at least in parishes with a low level of population. But as population densities increased to the point where it was no longer possible to know the needs of the inhabitants, the paternalistic approach broke down and was replaced by a more regulated system; some rural parishes even found it necessary to impose a legal assessment. At this stage they frequently tightened the requirement for granting relief. Burghs on the other hand were forced to resort to the use of assessments long before rural parishes. The greater density and larger number of people in urban areas meant that major reliance could not be placed upon the voluntary sources of funds, particularly in those burghs where church accommodation was acutely inadequate. The use of legal assessments in the burghs enabled the administration to be

more responsive to the needs of their poor and to meet the changing
circumstances caused by epidemics and economic depressions, by
guaranteeing a set amount available for distribution.

Generally, in rural parishes only individuals entitled by the
law to relief were granted assistance from the regular funds. But
ample evidence exists in the kirk session minutes that the able-
bodied employed also received assistance. It must be noted, however,
that such cases represent only a small proportion of the total
number of paupers. Moreover, the able-bodied were seldom granted
relief from the parochial funds during periods of unemployment. The
granting of occasional assistance to the able-bodied during times of
temporary sickness or personal disaster, such as the death of a
horse or cow, was more prevalent. Such aid was held to be a means
of preventing individuals from becoming regular paupers. The source
of funds for these distributions was the one-half of the church door
collections left to the disposal of the kirk sessions, hence
independent of the poor's funds. Relief in the burghs was generally
restricted to those legally entitled to it. The able-bodied,
whether in or out of work, were seldom granted assistance from the
public funds. These individuals in times of need were forced to
rely on the help of private charity, which fourished in Scotland's
major towns. Nonetheless, examples were found of the able-bodied
employed receiving assistance from the workhouse funds, as for
example when a wet nurse was provided to widowers.

The period 1745 to 1845 witnessed the break-down of the
traditional parochial system in most areas south of the Highland
line, with a fairly liberal paternalism being replaced by a harsher
system, one requiring a greater degree of formal regulation. Change
occurred first in the urban areas with the formation of workhouses,
which were frequently used as a means test. Even before 1800 the
pressures of urbanisation and industrialisation were so acute that

the major towns could not cope with the intensity of destitution by sole reliance upon the workhouses and it was necessary to introduce out-pensions. Similar patterns of change were experienced by the rural parishes near the larger towns and in the Borders. The role of the poor laws not only changed, but also the role of private charity, for it too became more institutionalised as the time period progressed.

The Scottish system of poor relief as compared to the English system was cheaper to administer, for there were few paid overseers and little emphasis on removal of paupers. The English system was wasteful due to administrative costs, especially the expenses resulting from the Settlement Acts. These items thus cause an overstatement of expenses per pauper for England as compared to Scotland. Little wonder then that the English envied the Scottish parochial system particularly with its greater degree of uniformity as a result of fewer administrative units.

The most famous defender of the Scottish poor laws was Rev. Dr. Thomas Chalmers, who attempted to restore the parochial concepts to a parish in Glasgow. His attempts were admired, but they also received extensive criticism from the administrators of relief in Glasgow. These administrators realised that the problems of destitution were too acute to place major emphasis for relief on the generosity of relatives and neighbours and voluntary sources of finance. The survival of an urban-industrial labour force depended upon organised assistance in times of severe need. Chalmers' St. John's experiment was not an unqualified success; yet, it produced admireable practices such as parochial visitation and education. But overall the experiment was idealistic and romantic and would have failed immediately if not for the magnetic personality of its founder.

The century under study was one of marked economic growth. The industrial belt of Glasgow-Edinburgh was by 1820 a major manufacturing centre within Britain. At the same time there was tremendous social displacement and a rise in the amount of destitution. Business cycles were a common feature of the day, with the resultant recessions creating large-scale unemployment. Ironically in a period of social upheaval serious debate concerning the humanity and importance of the Scottish poor law did not occur until after 1815. Indeed, even then such discussion that did take place largely failed to recognise that destitution was the result of trade fluctuations and not personal behaviour or morality. In the post-1815 period the existing tenets became an emotive rather than a rational topic of discussion. A particular view of the Highland ethos and a stress on the evils of assessment were notions tenaciously held. It is curious that the Scottish radical movements between 1816 and 1820 did not attempt, except in a few isolated cases, to establish a link with the poor. Perhaps the reason for this lay in the belief that the able-bodied unemployed should not be entitled to public relief was so ingrained in the minds of the Scots that any attempt to produce allowances for them were futile. Within this environment we find such individuals as Dr. Chalmers attempting to maintain the *status quo*, and indeed to return to the parochial system of rural Scotland. To be contrasted with Chalmers is W. P. Alison, who worked tirelessly to improve the conditions of the urban poor. An Alison in Scotland before 1800 would be hard to imagine. He was the product of a new wave of social consciousness sweeping Britain. He was instrumental in bringing about changes, though ones not as far-reaching as he proposed.

When changes finally came in Scottish poor law legislation in 1845, they were not the result of an upsurge of popular protest or the development of middle class humanitarianism, but were rather the product of fear and finance. Dr. Alison's appeals to legislators were potent because the fever epidemics of the 1830s, although based on poverty and malnutrition, also scorged the middle classes. Moreover, the Disruption of the Church of Scotland in 1843 placed a greater financial burden on the middle classes, as they were the ones who mainly stayed with the much reduced Established Church. The loyalists thus had an interest in helping the Church to divest itself of its role as poor law administrator. But the 1845 Poor Law Amendment Act (Scotland) was not symmetrical in its operation: it eased the pressures on the better off without improving the conditions of the poor. Only the shape of the system was changed, the basic philosophy remained. Little wonder then that private charity necessarily assumed a crucial role within Scotland; through it the condition of Scotland's poor was thus eased, to some degree compensating for the inadequacy of the legal provision made for them.

BIBLIOGRAPHY

Manuscripts:

Kirk Session Minutes:

    Ross and Cromarty: (a) Cromarty 1745-1845; (b) Kiltearn 1770-97,
                      1817-46
    Inverness: (a) Croy 1745-75, 1824-45; (b) Cawdor 1745-1828;
             (c) Moy 1745-1803, 1807-45.
    Bute: (a) Kilmory 1762-92, 1794-1845; (b) Rothesay 1800-45
    Argyle: (a) Craignish 1755-1835; (b) Kilmore 1766-1828;
          (c) Dunoon 1801-45
    Caithness: (a) Canisbay 1745-1845; (b) Halkirk 1781-1842;
             (c) Reay 1835-45
    Orkney: (a) Sandwick 1755-1842

    Elgin: (a) Drainie 1745-1815; (b) Elgin 1767-1843
    Banff: (a) Deskford 1745-1845; (b) Grange 1745-1845
    Aberdeen: (a) Kemnay 1745-1845; (b) Tough 1751-1845
    Kincardine: (a) Fordoun 1747-1845; (b) Nigg 1757-1845
    Forfar: (a) Craig 1758-1845
    Perth: (a) Aberfoyle 1773-1845; (b) Liff 1786-1845

    Fife: (a) Kilmany 1777-1844; (b) Anstruther Easter 1745-1845
    Kinross: (a) Arngask 1780-1845; (b) Orwell 1745-1845
    Haddington: (a) Salton 1745-1845; (b) Tranent 1745-1845;
              (c) Dalkeith 1745-1802
    Linlithgow: (a) Uphall 1745-1845; (b) Cramond 1745-1845
    Edinburgh: (a) Cranstoun 1783-1845; (b) Newbattle 1754-1845

    Stirling: (a) Falkirk 1753-1845; (b) Dunipace 1776-1845
    Dumbarton: (a) Cardross 1810-1845; (b) Arrochar 1764-1845
    Renfrew: (a) Eastwood 1745-1845
    Ayr: (a) Ballantrae 1745-81, 1815-45; (b) Sorn 1752-63, 1791-
        1830
    Lanark: (a) Shotts 1795-1845; (b) Bothwell 1754-89, 1813-27
        1837-45

    Berwick: (a) Ayton 1758-1845; (b) Lauder 1745-1845
    Peebles: (a) Manor 1745-1845; (b) Stobo 1754-1843
    Roxburgh: (a) Sprouston 1745-1845; (b) Hounan 1745-82, 1829-31
    Dumfries: (a) Tynron 1784-1845; (b) Dumfries 1745-1838
    Kirkcudbright: (a) Anwoth 1770-1836; (b) Kells 1745-1828
    Wigton: (a) Mochrum 1826-32; (b) Sorbie 1829-45

Urban Areas:

    Aberdeen: (a) Greyfriars 1828-45; (b) St. Nichols 1745-1845;
             (c) St. Nichols South 1828-45
    Dundee: (a) Chapelshade 1797-1844; (b) School Wynd (Dissent)
          1810-45
    Dumfries: (a) Buccleuch (Dissent) 1810-45
    Glasgow: (a) Glasgow General Session 1782-1828: (b) St. Paul's
          1786-1835; (c) St. Mungo's 1788-1846; (d) Tron 1790-
          1800; (e) Blackfriars 1797-1846; (f) St. George 1812-
          46; (g) St. John's 1819-45; (h) Greyfriars (Dissent)
          1745-50, 1801-45; (i) Great Hamilton (Dissent) 1795-
          1845; (j) Original (Dissent) 1808-41; (k) London Road
          (Dissent) 1838-45

Edinburgh: (a) Canongate 1745-1845; (b) St. Cuthbert's 1745-1845;
(c) Greyfriars Old 1775-1814, 1829-45; (d) Greyfriars
New 1839-45; (d) New Street 1834-45; (f) St.
Mary's 1825-45; (g) Trinity College 1830-45; (h) St.
Stephen's 1829-45; (i) Free Tron (Dissent) 1801-48
Paisley: (a) Abbey 1829-45

Note: The above records are housed in H.M. Register House, Edinburgh.

Heritors Records:

Perth: (a) Liff 1836-45

Kinross: (a) Arngask 1773-1845; (b) Orwell 1767-1845
Haddington: (a) Salton 1835-45; (b) Tranent 1753-1845;
(c) Dalkeith 1763-1845
Linlithgow: (a) Uphall 1829-45; (b) Cramond 1816-45
Edinburgh: (a) Newbattle 1745-57, 1807-45; (b) St. Cuthbert's
1773-1845

Stirling: (a) Falkirk 1788-1845; (b) Dunipace 1805-45
Dumbarton: (a) Cardross 1818-45
Renfrew: (a) Eastwood 1803-45; (b) Govan 1791-1845
Ayr: (a) Ballantrae 1826-45; (b) Sorn 1819-45
Lanark: (a) Shotts 1794-1845; (b) Bothwell 1756-1829;
(c) Paisley 1785-1831

Berwick: (a) Ayton 1835-45; (b) Lauder 1745-1845
Peebles: (a) Manor 1829-41; (b) Stobo 1840-45
Roxburgh: (a) Sprouston 1808-43; (b) Hounam 1749-1845
Dumfries: (a) Tynron 1839-45
Kirkcudbright: (a) Anwoth 1825-45; (b) Kells 1786-1845

Note: The above records are housed in H.M. Register House, Edinburgh.

Town Council Minutes:

Glasgow
Edinburgh
Dumfries
Inverness
Dundee

Workhouse Minutes:

Edinburgh Charity Workhouse (Edinburgh City Archives)
Canongate Charity Workhouse (Edinburgh City Archives)
St. Cuthbert's Charity Workhouse (Edinburgh City Archives)
Glasgow Town's Hospital (Mitchell Library)
Paisley Town's Hospital (H.M. Register House)
Dalkeith Charity Workhouse (H.M. Register House)
Dumfries Muirhead's Hospital (Private holding)

Act of the General Church-Sessions of Edinburgh anent the Poor, 6th June,
1732. (Edinburgh University Library)

Act of the Town-Council of Edinburgh, 9th February, 1774. (National
Library of Scotland)

Chalmers Papers. (New College Library, Edinburgh)

Chalmers, Thomas. "Reflections of 1839 on the now protracted experience of Pauperism in Glasgow - The experience of twenty years, which began in 1815, and terminated in 1837". Manuscript, Mitchell Library.

Clark, John letter to W. P. Alison, 14th April, 1845. (Edinburgh University Library)

Fettercairn Papers. (National Library of Scotland)

Moncrieff, James letter to Edinburgh Town Council, 28th July, 1823. (Edinburgh City Archives)

Mure of Caldwell Papers. (National Library of Scotland)

Regulations of Edinburgh Charity Workhouse, 1750. (Edinburgh City Archives)

Robertson, Robert letter to Mr Thomson, Inspector of Poor, Canongate, 30th April, 1839. (Edinburgh University Library)

Robert Scott Moncrieff Letters, Royal Bank of Scotland, 1801-07. (National Commercial Banking Group, Edinburgh)

Seaforth Estate. (H.M. Register House)

Parliamentary Papers:

Board of Agriculture Reports: Aberdeen (1811), Ayr (1811), Berwick (1809), Dumfries (1912), Kincardine (1810), Peebles (1802), Renfrew (1812), Ross and Cromarty (1810), West-Lothian (1811)

Third Report from the Select Committee on the Poor Law with an appendix containing Returns from the General Assembly of the Church of Scotland, 1818.

Report from the Select Committee of the House of Commons on the Observance of the Lord's Day; with Extracts from the Evidence taken by that Committee, 1832.

First Report of the Commissioners of Religious Instruction, Scotland, 1837.

Report by a Committee of the General Assembly on the Management of the Poor in Scotland, 1839.

Children's Employment Commission: First Report of the Commissioners, Mines, 1842.

Reports on the Sanitary Condition of the Labouring Population of Scotland, 1842. Inverness, Glasgow, Easter Ross, Edinburgh, Lanark, Aberdeen, Musselburgh and Inveresk.

Select Committee on the Destitute Inhabitants of Paisley, 1843.

Report from Her Majesty's Commissioners for Inquiry into the Administration and Practical Operation of the Poor Law in Scotland, 1844.

Royal Commission on the Poor Laws and Relief of Distress.   Report on
    Scotland, 1909.

Newspapers and Periodicals:

The Aberdeen Almanac and Northern Register

The Bee

The Cheap Magazine

The Christian Journal of the United Presbyterian Church

Edinburgh Advertiser

Edinburgh Correspondent

The Edinburgh Encyclopaedia

Edinburgh Weekly Journal

The Emmet

Encyclopaedia Britannica

Glasgow Courant

Glasgow Courier

Glasgow Herald

The Glasgow Magazine and Clydesdale Monthly Register

Glasgow Mercury

The Literary Museum and Critical Review

The Monthly Monitor and Philanthropic Museum

Scots Times

Scotsman

Reformers Gazette

Contemporary Books and Pamphlets to 1850:

Acts of the General Assembly of the Church of Scotland, 1638-1842.
    Edinburgh: Edinburgh Printing and Publishing Co., 1843.

The Acts of the Parliaments of Scotland. Printed by command of His
    Majesty King George III., 1814.

Adams, Alex Maxwell. *Observations on the Mode of Administering the
    Poor Laws at the Town's Hospital, Glasgow.* 1847.

Alison, Archibald. *The Principles of Population, and Their Connection
    with Human Happiness.* Edinburgh: William Blackwood and Sons,
    1840.

Alison, S. Scott. *Report on the Sanitary [sic] Condition and General
    Economy of the Town of Tranent, and the Neighbouring District
    in Haddingtonshire.* 1840.

Alison, W. P. *Observations on the Management of the Poor in Scotland,
    and its effects on the Health of the Great Towns.* Edinburgh:
    William Blackwood and Sons, 1840.

_____. *Reply to the Pamphlet Entitled "Proposed Alteration of the Scottish Poor Law Considered and Commented on: by David Monypenny, Esp., of Pitmilly."* Edinburgh: William Blackwood and Sons, 1840.

_____. *Reply to Dr. Chalmers' Objections to an Improvement of the Legal Provision for the Poor in Scotland.* Edinburgh: William Blackwood and Sons, 1841.

_____. *Remarks on the Report of Her Majesty's Commissioners on the Poor-Laws of Scotland, presented to Parliament in 1844, and on the Dissent of Mr Twisleton from that Report.* Edinburgh: William Blackwood and Sons, 1844.

Anon. (Dr. Crawford). *The Attic Stories, or the opinions of Edward Hazelrig, Esq.* Glasgow: James Hedderwick, 1818.

Anon. *Brief Statement of Facts respecting the Edinburgh Charity Workhouse.* Edinburgh: 1840.

Anon. *The Causes of Pauperism and Crime.* Edinburgh: John Anderson, 1834.

Anon. *Glasgow-Polity displayed: or, a Review of a late Publication, Entitled, A Letter to the Citizens of Glasgow; said to contain a short view of the Management of the Poor's Funds, under the administration of the General-Session.* Glasgow: Town and Country, 1785.

Anon. *Letter addressed to the Right Hon. Sir Robert Peel, Bart. on the Poor-Law System of Scotland, with a view to such alterations as may shortly be brought before Parliament.* Edinburgh: William Blackwood and Sons, 1845.

Anon. *A Letter on the Nature, Extent, and Management, of Poor Rates in Scotland: with a Review of the Controversy respecting the Abolition of Poor Laws.* Edinburgh: John Park, 1807.

Anon. *Observations on the Causes and Remedies of Destitution in the Highlands of Scotland.* Glasgow: John Smith and Son, 1837.

Association for Obtaining an Official Inquiry into the Pauperism of Scotland. Edinburgh: 23rd March, 1840.

Baillie, Rev. John, ed. *Report of the Proceedings in the General Assembly of the Church of Scotland for 1841.* Edinburgh: John Johnstone, 1841.

Begg, J. *Report in regard to the State of Pauperism in the Parish of Liberton, with Suggestions for Improving It; submitted to the Heritors by the Kirk Session, November 1839.* Edinburgh: John Johnstone, 1839.

Buchanan, Moses Steven. *History of the Glasgow Royal Infirmary.* Glasgow: James Lumsden and Sons, 1832.

Burns, Rev. Robert. *Historical Dissertations on the Law and Practice of Great Britain, and particularly of Scotland, with Regard to the Poor.* Glasgow: Young, Gallie, and Company, 1819.

Burton, John Hill. *A Manual of the Law of Scotland, Civil, Municipal, Criminal, and Ecclesiastical; with a Practical Commentary on the Mercantile Law,. and on the Powers and duties of Justices of the Peace and other Magistrates.* Edinburgh: Oliver and Boyd, 1839.

Caird, Alexander M'Neel. *The Poor Law Manual, containing the New Poor Law Act.* Edinburgh: Adam and Charles Black, 1846.

Chalmers, Thomas. *Considerations on the System of Parochial Schools in Scotland, and on the Advantage of Establishing them in Large Towns.* Glasgow: James Hedderwick, 1819.

_____. *A Speech Delivered on the 24th May, 1822, Before the General Assembly of the Church of Scotland.* 1822.

_____. *Sermons Preached in St. John's Church, Glasgow.* Glasgow: Chalmers and Collins, 1823.

_____. *Statement in Regard to the Pauperism of Glasgow, from the Experience of the Last Eight Years.* Glasgow: Chalmers and Collins, 1823.

_____. *The Christian and Civic Economy of Large Towns.* Glasgow: Chalmers and Collins, 1823.

_____. *On Political Economy, in connexion with the Moral State and Moral Prospects of Society.* Glasgow: William Collins, n.d.

_____. *On the Sufficiency of the Parochial System, without a Poor Rate, for the Right Management of the Poor.* Glasgow: William Collins, 1841.

_____. *On the Economics of the Free Church of Scotland.* Edinburgh: John D. Love, 1846.

Circular from the Managers of the Edinburgh Charity Workhouse to their Constituents. 1st January, 1844.

City of Edinburgh. *Pensions for the Poor of the City, 1719-44.*

Cleghorn, James. *Thoughts on the expediency of a General Provident Institution, for the Benefit of the Working Classes.* Edinburgh: John Hutchison, 1824.

Cleland, James. *Description of the Ten Parishes into which the City of Glasgow was Divided, in the year 1820, exhibiting the Population in each Parish: and a Description of the Twenty-four Police Wards.* James Hedderwick, 1820.

_____. *Statistical Tables Relative to the City of Glasgow, with other matters therewith connected.* Glasgow: James Lumsden and Son, 1823.

_____. *The Rise and Progress of the City of Glasgow, comprising an account of Its Public Buildings, Charitable Institutions, and other Establishments, till the year M.DCCC.XX.* Glasgow: John Smith and Son, 1824.

_____. *Maintenance of the Poor in Glasgow.* 1828.

_____. *Enumeration of the Inhabitants of the City of Glasgow and County of Lanark. For the Government Census of M.DCCC.XXXI. with Population and Statistical Tables Relative to England and Scotland.* Glasgow: John Smith and Son, 1832.

_____. *Letter to His Grace the Duke of Hamilton and Brandon, respecting the Parochial Registers of Scotland.* Glasgow: University Press, 1834.

_____. *Statistical Facts Descriptive of the Former and Present State of Glasgow.* Glasgow: Bell and Bain, 1837.

Collins, William. *Statistics of the Church Accommodation of Glasgow, Barony, and Gorbals.* Glasgow: William Collins, 1836.

Cook, John. *A Brief view of the Scottish Systems for the Relief of the Poor; and of some Proposed Changes on it.* Edinburgh: John Johnstone, 1841.

Cowan, Robert. *Vital Statistics of Glasgow, Illustrating the Sanitary Condition of the Population.* 1840.

Craig, Alexander. *Memoir Regarding the Law of Settlement of Paupers in Scotland, submitted to the Consideration of the Managers for the Poor of St. Cuthbert, or West Kirk Parish.* Edinburgh: Adam and Charles Black, 1841.

Craig, James. *Report of the General Kirk-Sessions of Edinburgh, anent the Establishment by Law of a Fund for the Maintenance and Employment of the Poor.* 1749.

Cruickshank, James. *Observations on the Scotch System of Poor Laws; together with the explanation of a plan for the suppression of Vagrants, Street Beggars, and Impostors; for the Relief of occasional distress; and the Encouragement of Industry among the Poor.* Aberdeen: F. Frost, 1813.

Drysdale, W. *Notes for Conferences respecting the Annuity, Poor's Money, &c.* Edinburgh, 1829.

Eden, Sir Frederic Morton. *The State of the Poor.* London: J. Davis, 1797.

Ewing, James. *Report for the Directors of the Town's Hospital of Glasgow on the Management of the City Poor, the Suppression of Mendicity, and the principles of the plan for the new Hospital.* Glasgow: E. Chapman, 1818.

Extracts from Letters to the Rev. Dr. M'Leod, Glasgow, Regarding the Famine and Destitution in the Highlands and Islands of Scotland. Glasgow: John Smith and Son, 1847.

Extracts from Letters transmitted by Clergymen, Magistrates, and others, relative to the present Destitution in the Highland and Islands of Scotland. London: Richard Watts, 1837.

Extracts from the Minutes and Proceedings of the Heritors and Kirk-Session of the Parish of St. Cuthbert's. Edinburgh: Anderson and Bryce, 1833.

Ferrie, Robert and others. *Poor Rates of Glasgow.* 1830.

First Report of the Managers for the Poor of the Parish of St. Cutherbert's or West Kirk. Edinburgh: Anderson and Bryce, 1834.

Forbes, J. H. *Report of the Committee, to whom it was remitted to suggest a plan for affording Relief to the Labouring Classes in the City and Suburbs.* Edinburgh: Alex. Smellie, 1816.

Fullarton, Allan and Charles R. Baird. *Remarks on the Evils at Present Affecting the Highlands and Islands of Scotland; with Some Suggestions as to Their Remedies.* Glasgow: William Collins, 1838.

Gairdner, Andrew. *Historical Account of the Old People's Hospital, Commonly called, the Trinity Hospital in Edinburgh; also, Proposals how to raise a Fund for the Maintenance of Widows and Orphans, under the Title of a Charity-Bank.* Edinburgh: 1728.

Gibb, Rev. Dr. Gavin. *Answers to the Queries of the General Assembly of the Church of Scotland concerning the Management of the Poor in Glasgow.* Glasgow: 1817.

Haldane, Rev. Dr. *Remarks on a Report by a Committee Appointed by the Town Council of St. Andrews to Inquire into the Condition of the Poor in that City.* Cupar-Fife: Fifeshire Journal Office, 1840.

Hamilton, Robert. *An Address to the Inhabitants of Aberdeen on the Management of the Poor; with statements of the income and expenditure of the United Fund, from 1813 to 1821, Inclusive.* Aberdeen: D. Chalmers and Co., 1822.

Interlocutor and Note in Cause Royal Bank against the Charity Work-House. Edinburgh: Neill and Company, 1843.

Lees, James. *A Treatise on the Poor Laws of Scotland, as now regulated by the Poor Law Amendment Act and the Instructions of the Board of Supervision.* Edinburgh: Edinburgh Printing and Publishing Company, 1847.

Lewis. Rev. G. *The Pauper Bill of Dundee, and what Should be Done with It.* Dundee: W. Middleton, 1841.

List of Out-pensioners of the Charity Workhouse of Edinburgh, 1843.

McFarlan, John. *Inquiries Concerning the Poor.* Edinburgh: J. Dickson, 1782.

MacFarlan, John F. *Inquiry Respecting the Sobriety and Steadiness of the Working Classes.* Edinburgh: William Tait, 1834.

MacGill, Stevenson. "On Provision for the Poor of Glasgow," in *Discourses and Essays on Subjects of Public Interest.* 1819.

McLaren, D. *Report of the Treasurer's Committee, to the Town-Council of Edinburgh, on remit to Consider and Report regarding the best means of obtaining immediate accommodation for Pauper Lunatics.* Edinburgh: H. and J. Pillans, 1837.

166.

Maclure, David. *Eight Letters on the Administration of Relief to the Poor of Glasgow.* Glasgow: David Chambers, 1848.

McNeill, Duncan and A. Dunlap. *Case for the Lord Provost, Magistrates, and Council of the City of Edinburgh regarding the Constitution of the Charity Workhouse; with opinion thereon.* Edinburgh: Thomas Allan and Co., 1842.

Managers of Orphan Hospital. *An Historical Account of the Orphan Hospital of Edinburgh.* Edinburgh: J. and C. Muirhead, 1833.

Memorandum for the Lord Provost, Magistrates, and Town-Council, from the Managers of the Edinburgh Charity Work-House, relative to the erection of a New Children's Hospital. Edinburgh: Neill and Co., 1842.

Memorial, respecting the Charity-Workhouse of Edinburgh. Edinburgh: 22nd December, 1774.

Millar, Richard. *Statements Relative to the Present Prevalence of Epidemic Fever among the Poorer Classes of Glasgow: together with some suggestions, both for affording more adequate assistance to the sick, and for checking the further progress of the contagion.* Glasgow: John Smith and Son, 1818.

Minute of the Committee Relative to the Suppression of Common begging, and relieving of the Industrious and Destitute Poor, 8th December, 1812. Edinburgh: 1812.

Monilaws, Rev. George Hope. *A Catechism on Pauperism and the Poor-Laws in Scotland.* Edinburgh: William Blackwood and Sons, 1845.

Monypenny, David. *Remarks on the Poor Laws, and the Method of Providing for the Poor, in Scotland.* Edinburgh: Thomas Clark, 1836.

_____. *Proposed Alteration of the Scottish Poor Laws, and the Administration Thereof, as stated by Dr. Alison, in his "Observations on the Management of the Poor in Scotland", considered and Commented on.* Edinburgh: William Whyte and Co., 1840.

_____. *Additional Remarks on the Proposed Alteration of the Scottish Poor Laws, and of the Administration Thereof.* Edinburgh: William Whyte and Co., 1841.

Morison, William Maxwell, ed. *The Decisions of the Court of Session, from its institution until the separation of the Court into two Divisions in the year 1808, digested under proper heads, in the form of a dictionary.* Edinburgh: Archibald Constable and Company, 1811.

The New Statistical Account of Scotland. Edinburgh: William Blackwood and Sons, 1845.

The Parliamentary Debates. Published under the superintendence of T. C. Hansard.

Penny, W. *Proposed Alteration in the Management of the Poor of Edinburgh.* Edinburgh: 1834.

Perry, Robert. *Facts and Observations on the Sanitary State of Glasgow During the last year; with Statistical Tables on the late epidemic, showing the connection existing between Poverty, Disease, and Crime.* Glasgow: 1844.

Pusey, Ph. *The Poor in Scotland; compiled from the Evidence Taken before the Scotch Poor-Law Commission.* London: James Burns, 1844.

Ranken, Andrew. *A Letter Addressed to the Rev. Dr. Chalmers, occasioned by His frequent allusions to the "Impregnable Minds of Certain Conveners and Councilmen", on the Subject of Pauperism in the City of Glasgow; accompanied with official documents.* Glasgow: James Hedderwick and Son, 1830.

Regulations for the Town's Hospital of Glasgow: with an Introduction, containing a view of the History of the Hospital, and the Management of the Poor. Glasgow: Glasgow Courier Co., 1830.

Report by the Committee Appointed by the Town Council of St. Andrews to Inquire into the Condition of the Poor in the Parishes of St. Andrews and St. Leonards. St. Andrews: 28th August, 1840.

Report of the Committee appointed by the Commissioners of Police, to inquire into the Practicability of suppressing the practice of Common Begging, and relieving the Industrious and Destitute Poor. Edinburgh: Alex. Lawrie and Co., 1812.

Report of the Committee Appointed at a Meeting of the Commissioners of Police, and other Inhabitants of the City of Edinburgh, held on the 8th December, 1812, when it was unanimously resolved; - "That it was wise and expedient that a Society be formed to suppress the Practice of Common Begging, and relieving the Industrious and Destitute Poor;" and to whom a Remit was made to draw up a Report of a plan for that Purpose. Edinburgh: Alex. Lawrie and Co., 1813.

Report of Committee appointed by the Parochial Board, to examine as to which of the Three Modes of Rating, Prescribed in the Act of 8 and 9 Vict. Cap. 83 ought to be adopted in the City Parish of Glasgow. Glasgow: David Maclure, 1847.

Report of the Committee appointed by the Quarterly Meeting of the Town's Hospital, on the 19th November last, to inquire into and report on the state of the Hospital. Glasgow: Jack and Callie, 1816.

Report of the Committee of the Kirk-Session and Heritors of the Parish of St. Cuthbert's or West-Kirk; containing the Resolutions proposed for the future Management of the Charity Work-House, and Funds belonging to the Poor. Edinburgh: Anderson and Bryce, 1833.

Report of the First Annual General Meeting of the Governors of the New Town Dispensary. Edinburgh: Caw and Elder, 1817.

Report to the Guildry of the City of Edinburgh, by their Eighteen Representatives at the Board of Management of the Edinburgh Charity Workhouse. Edinburgh: 1844.

Report of the Law and Treasurer's Committees, to the Town Council of Edinburgh, on remits regarding the affairs of the Charity Workhouse. Edinburgh: J. and C. Muirhead, 1838.

Report of Lunatic Asylum. Glasgow: 1814.

A Report of the Present State of the Charity Work-House of Edinburgh. Edinburgh: 1773.

A Report of the State of the Dumfries Hospital or Poor's-House for the Year Ending at Martinmas, 1814.

Report of the Sub-Committee appointed by the Law Committee of the Town-Council in regard to the affairs of the Charity Workhouse. Edinburgh: Neill and Co., 9th January, 1841.

Report by the Treasurer's Committee on Memorial from the Managers of the Charity Work-House, regarding the Assessment for the Current Year. Edinburgh: Neill and Co., 1842.

Resolutions of the Kirk-Session and Heritors of the Parish of St. Cuthbert's for the Future Management of the Charity Work-House, and Funds belonging to the Poor, agreed upon and adopted. Edinburgh: Anderson and Bryce, 1833.

Revised Report of the Sub-Committee Appointed by the Law Committee of the Town-Council in regard to the affairs of the Charity Workhouse. Edinburgh: Neill and Co., 9th March, 1841.

Robertson, H. and others. *Report of the Committee of Council, appointed to consider the Applications for and against a change in the present mode of apportioning the assessment for the Maintenance of the poor; and proceeding of Council thereon.* Glasgow: Hutchison and Brookman, 1829.

Rules and Regulations for the Edinburgh Charity Work-House. Edinburgh: Balfour and Jack, 1842.

Second Report of the Committee of the Association for Obtaining an Official Inquiry into the Pauperism of Scotland. Edinburgh: William Blackwood and Sons, 1841.

A Short Account of the Town's Hospital in Glasgow with the Regulations and Abstracts of the Expenses for the First Eight Years. Glasgow: 1742.

Sinclair, Sir John, ed. *The Statistical Account of Scotland.* Edinburgh: William Creech, 1797.

State of the Present Funds of the Charity Work-House of the City of Edinburgh; and Proposals for applying to the Legislature for an Act of Parliament, for establishing a more equal and certain Fund for the Maintenance and Support of the Begging Poor, and Outpensioners of the said City. 1748.

Statement on behalf of the Committee of Subscribers for promoting a change in the Mode of Assessment for the Poor of the City of Glasgow. Glasgow: Hutchison and Brookman, 1831.

Statement from the Session of St. John's Parish, Glasgow, to the Directors of the Town's Hospital, in regard to the Management of Their Poor. Glasgow: 1836.

Statement of the Question Between the Heritors of the Parish of St. Cuthbert's, or West Kirk, and the Kirk-Session of that Parish. Edinburgh: R. Marshall, 1835.

Stark, William. *Considerations Addressed to the Heritors and Kirk-Sessions of Scotland, particularly of the Border Counties, on Certain Questions Connected with the Administration of the Affairs of the Poor.* Edinburgh: Waugh and Innes, 1826.

Strickland, George. *A Discourse on the Poor Laws of England and Scotland, on the State of the Poor of Ireland, and on Emigration.* London: James Ridgway, 1827.

Summons of Reduction and Declarator - The Lord Provost, Magistrates and Council of the City of Edinburgh; against the Managers and Directors of the Edinburgh Charity Work-House. 17th April, 1843.

Supplementary Report on the State of the Poor in Berwickshire. Edinburgh: Neill and Co., 1842.

Tod, Thomas. *Observations on Dr. M'Farlan's Inquiries Concerning the State of the Poor.* Edinburgh: James Donaldson, 1783.

_____. *A Short Account of the Charitable Institutions in Edinburgh.* Edinburgh: 1785.

Tufnell, E. C. "Report on Scotland", in *Poor Law Commission Report*, Appendix A, 2-3, 1834.

Walker, W. S. *A Practical Analysis of the Act 8 and 9 Victoria, Cap. 83, for the Amendment and Better Administration of the Laws Relating to the Relief of the Poor in Scotland.* Edinburgh: William Blackwood and Sons, 1845.

Wardlaw, Ralph. *An Essay on Benevolent Associations for the Relief of the Poor.* Glasgow: Young, Gallie and Co., 1818.

Weir, James. *An Essay on the Legal Right of the Poor to Relief.* Stirling; The Journal Office, 1833.

Williamson, Joseph. *Memorial for the Magistrates and Council of the City of Edinburgh, containing a Short Account of the Erection of the Charity Work-House, the Reasons for applying to the Legislature, in order to procure the Establishment of a Certain and equal Fund for the Maintenance and Employment of Poor belonging to this City and Royalty.* 1749.

Wood, A. and W. Penny. *Memorial and Queries for the Managers of the Edinburgh Charity Work-House. And Opinion Thereon.* Edinburgh: E. & J. Pillans, 1842.

170.

Articles to 1850:

Alison, W. P. "Illustrations of the Practical Operation of the
Scottish System of Management of the Poor", in *Quarterly Journal
of the Statistical Society of London*, vol. 3, October, 1840.

_____. "Further Illustrations of the Practical Operation of
the Scotch System of Management of the Poor", in *Journal of the
Statistical Society of London*, January, 1842.

_____. "Observations on the Generation of Fever", in
*Reports on the Sanitary Condition of the Labouring population of
Scotland*. London: W. Clowes and Sons, 1842.

_____. "On the Destitution and Mortality in some of the
Large Towns in Scotland", in *Journal of the Statistical Society
of London*, vol. 5, 1842.

_____. "Notes on the Report of the Royal Commissioners on
the Operation of the Poor Laws in Scotland, 1844", in *Journal of
the Statistical Society of London*, vol. 7, 1844.

_____. "Report on the Medical Relief of the Parochial Poor
of Scotland, under the former Poor Law", in *Journal of the
Statistical Society of London*, vol. 9, 1846.

Anon. "Review of 'Report from the Select Committee on the Poor-Laws,
with the Minutes of Evidence taken before the Committee'", in
The Edinburgh Review, vol. 29th February, 1818.

Anon. "Review of 'Statement in Regard to the Pauperism of Glasgow,
from the Experience of the last Eight Years' by Thomas Chalmers",
in *Edinburgh Review*, vol, 41, 1824-5.

Baird, C. R. "Observations upon the Poorest Class of Operatives in
Glasgow in 1837", in *Journal of the Statistical Society of
London*, vol. 1, 1838-9.

Buchanan, Andrew. "Report of the Diseases which prevailed among the
Poor of Glasgow, during the summer of 1830", in *Glasgow Medical
Journal*, 1830, vol. 3.

Heriot, James. "Report of the State of the Poor in Fifeshire, and on
the Manner in which the Laws are Administered in the Several
Parishes of the County, and on the Effects of the present Poor
Laws", in *Journal of Agriculture*, 1843-5.

J.H.B.[Burton]. "Poor Laws and Pauperism in Scotland", in
Westminster Review, vol. XXXVI, October, 1841.

Macfarlane, John. "Report of the Diseases which prevaled among the
Poor of Glasgow, during the Autumn of 1827", in *Glasgow Medical
Journal*, 1830, vol. 1, pp. 97-109.

Other Works Post 1850:

*Appeal to the Inhabitants of Edinburgh by the Acting Committee of the
Edinburgh Association for the Improvement of the Condition of the
Poor.* 1868.

Black, William George. *A Handbook of Scottish Parochial Law other than Ecclesiastical.* Edinburgh: William Green and Sons, 1893.

Caird, Alexander N'Neel. *Special Evils of the Scottish Poor-Law.* Edinburgh: Edmonston and Douglas, 1877.

Caldwell, David. *Poor Law Administration: History of Parish of Ayr, from 1756 to 1895.* Ayr: "Observer" Office, n.d.

Campbell, Dugald. *Pauperism and the Poor Laws: A Letter to E.H.J. Crawford.* Greenock: Orr, Pollock and Co., 1869.

Checkland, S. G. and E. O. A., ed. *Report of the Royal Commission on the Poor Laws, 1834.* Harmondsworth: Penguin Books, 1974.

Checkland, E. O. A. *Philanthropy in Victorian Scotland.* Edinburgh: John Donald, 1980.

Cockburn, Henry. *Letters Chiefly connected with the Affairs of Scotland, from Henry Cockburn to Thomas Francis Kennedy, M.P.* London: William Ridgway, 1874.

Coode, George. *Report to the Poor Law Board on the Law of Settlement and Removal of the Poor.* London: 1851.

Cormack, Alexander A. *Poor Relief in Scotland: An Outline of the Growth and Administration of the Poor Laws in Scotland, from the Middle Ages to the Present Day.* Aberdeen: D. Wyllie and Son, 1923.

Curror, David. *Letter to the Right Honourable William Chamber of Glenormiston, Lord Provost of the City of Edinburgh, on the Aims and Practical Working of the Association, more Especially in reference to the Employment of the Poor.* 1868.

_____. *The Scottish Poor Law, and some contrasts Between its Principles and the Practices that have Grown upon it.* Edinburgh: Seton and Mackenzie, 1869.

Dunlop, Alexander Murray. *The Law of Scotland Regarding the Poor.* Edinburgh: William Blackwood and Sons, 1854.

Encyclopaedia of the Laws of Scotland. vol. XI, 1930.

Gibson, Henry J.C. *Dundee Royal Infirmary 1798-1948: The Story of the Old Infirmary.* Dundee: William Kidd and Sons, Ltd., 1948.

Glaister, John. *The Epidemic History of Glasgow during the Century 1783-1883.* Read before the Philosophical Society of Glasgow, 14th April, 1886.

Glasse, John. *Pauperism in Scotland, Past and Present.* Glasgow: Scottish National Committee for the Prevention of Destitution, 1910.

Graham, Henry Gray. *The Social Life of Scotland in the Eighteenth Century.* London: Adam and Charles Black, 1899.

Handbook of Glasgow Charitable and Beneficent Institutions, 1907.

Hanna, Rev. William. *Memoirs of the Life and Writings of Thomas Chalmers, D.D., LL.D.* Edinburgh: A. Fullarton and Co., 1852.

_____. *A Selection from the Correspondence of the Late Thomas Chalmers, D.D. LL.D.* Edinburgh: Thomas Constable and Co., 1853.

Harper, J. Wilson. *The Social Ideal and Dr. Chalmers' Contribution to Christian Economics.* Edinburgh: MacNiven and Wallace, 1910.

Hay, William. *Decisions on the Poor Law of Scotland in the Court of Session, and Awards by Arbitration.* Edinburgh: T. and T. Clark, 1859.

Hunter, Henry, ed. *Problems of Poverty, Selections from the Economic and Social Writings of Thomas Chalmers. D.D.* London: Thomas Nelson and Sons, 1912.

Kyde, James Gray. *Scottish Population Statistics including Webster's Analysis of Population 1755.* Edinburgh: T. and A. Constable, Ltd, 1952.

Lamond, Robert Peel. *The Scottish Poor Laws: Their History, Policy and Operation.* Glasgow: William Hodge and Co., 1892.

Levitt, I. A. and T. C. Smout. *The State of the Scottish Working Class in 1843.* Edinburgh: Scottish Academic Press, 1979.

MacKay, George A. *Management and Construction of Poorhouses and Almhouses.* Edinburgh: William Green and Sons, 1908.

MacKenzie, J. *On Pauperism - its cure; and the Land Question.* Edinburgh: Seton and MacKenzie, 1870.

McPherson, J. M. *The Kirk's Care of the Poor, with special reference to the North-East of Scotland.* Aberdeen: John Avery and Co., Ltd., n.d.

Mair, William. *A Digest of Laws and Decisions, Ecclesiastical and Civil, relating to the Constitution, Practice, and Affairs of the Church of Scotland.* Edinburgh: William Blackwood and Sons, 1895.

Marshall, Dorothy. *The English Poor in the Eighteenth Century. A Study in Social and Administrative History.* London: Routledge and Kegan Paul, Ltd., 1926.

Marshall, J. D. *The Old Poor Law, 1795-1834.* London: Macmillan, 1968.

Masterman, N., ed. *Chalmers on Charity. A Selection of Passages and Scenes to illustrate the Social Teaching and Practical Work of Thomas Chalmers, D.D.* Westminster: Archibald Constable and Co., 1900.

Mechie, Stewart. *The Church and Scottish Social Development, 1780-1870.* London: Oxford University Press, 1960.

Nicholls, Sir George. *A History of the English Poor Law, in Connexion with the Legislation and other circumstances affecting the condition of the People.* London: John Murray, 1854.

Parochial Board of Edinburgh: *Contract of Agreement, the Lord Provost, Magistrates, and Town Council, and the Ministers and Kirk Sessions of the City of Edinburgh for Building and Endowing the Charity Workhouse, 1740. Grant by the Said Lord Provost, Magistrates, and Town Council, to the Managers of the Poor. And Excerpts of Minutes of Meetings of the above, and other Public Bodies relative to the Poorhouse.* 1857.

Poynter, J. R. *Society and Pauperism: English Ideas on Poor Relief, 1795-1834.* London: Routledge and Kegan Paul, 1969.

Reid, John Alexander. *Digest of Decisions relating to the Poor Law of Scotland.* Edinburgh: Duncan Grant, 1880.

Rose, Michael E. *The English Poor Law, 1780-1930.* Newton Abbot: David and Charles, 1971.

Smith, John Guthrie. *A Digest of the Law of Scotland relating to the Poor, the Public Health, and other matters managed by Parochial Boards.* Edinburgh: T. and T. Clark, 1878.

Smout, T. C. *A History of the Scottish People 1560-1830.* London: Collins, 1969.

_____, ed. *The Search for Wealth and Stability.* London: Macmillan, 1979.

Strathesk, John (John Tod). *Hawkie: The Autobiography of a Gangrel.* Glasgow: David Robertson and Co., 1888.

Tate, W. E. *The Parish Chest,* 3rd ed. Cambridge: The University Press, 1969.

Taylor, Geoffrey. *The Problem of Poverty, 1660-1834.* London: Longmans, Green and Co., Ltd., 1969.

Walker, Alexander. *The History of the Workhouse or Poor's Hospital of Aberdeen from 1739 to 1818, its Boys' Hospital from 1818 to 1852, Girls' Hospital from 1828 to 1852 and its Boys' and Girls' Hospitals from 1852 to 1885.* Aberdeen: J. and J. P. Edmond and Spark, 1885.

Wilson, Alexander. *The Chartist Movement in Scotland.* Manchester: University Press, 1970.

Wood, Alexander. *The Scottish Poor Law, examined in its Principles and Tried by its results. With suggestion of remedies.* Edinburgh: Seton and MacKenzie, 1869.

Wood, Grace. *Dr. Chalmers and the Poor Laws. A Comparison of Scotch and English Pauperism and Evidence Before the Committee of the House of Commons.* Edinburgh: David Douglas, 1911.

Wright, Leslie C. *Scottish Chartism,* Edinburgh: Oliver and Boyd, Ltd., 1953.

Articles Post 1850:

Ashton, T. S. "The Standard of Life of the Workers in England, 1790-1830", in *JEH,* vol. 9, suppt., 1949.

Brown, Isabel. "A Short Account of the Town's Hospital in Glasgow", in *The Bibliotheck*, vol. 1, No. 1, Autumn, 1956.

Cage, R. A. "Debate: The Making of the Old Scottish Poor Law", in *Past and Present*, November, 1975.

Cage, R. A. and E. O. A. Checkland, "Thomas Chalmers and Urban Poverty: The St. John's Parish Experiment in Glasgow, 1819-1837", in *Philosophical Journal*, Spring, 1976.

Fishlow, Albert. "The Trustee Savings Banks, 1817-1861", in *JEH*, 1961, vol. XXI, no. 1.

Gourvish, T. R. "The Cost of Living in Glasgow in the Early Nineteenth Century", in *EcHR*, second series, vol. 25, February, 1972.

Grey, H. "Economic Welfare and Money Incomes in the Highlands, 1750-1850", in *SJPE*, vol. 2, February, 1955.

Hamilton, Lord George. "A Statistical Survey of the Problems of Pauperism", in *Journal of the Royal Statistical Society*, LXXXIV, 1910-11.

Kerr, R. and J. R. Lockie. "Scottish Beggars' Badges", in *Proceedings of the Society of Antiquaries of Scotland*, 1961-62, vol. XCV.

Leeming, F. A. "Social Accounting and the Old Statistical Account", in *Scottish Geographical Magazine*, LXXIX, 1963.

Loch, C. S. "Poor Relief in Scotland: its Statistics and Development, 1791 to 1891", in *Journal of the Royal Statistical Society*, vol. LXI, June, 1898.

McKay, Johnston R. (Jr.) "The Disruption: An Examination of Some Statistics", in *The Philosophical Journal*, vol. 6, No. 2, 1969.

Mason, John. "Scottish Charity Schools of the Eighteenth Century", in *SHR*, vol. XXXIII, no. 115, April, 1954.

Mitchison, R. "The Making of the Old Scottish Poor Law", in *P&P*, May, 1974.

Morgan, Valerie. "Agricultural Wage Rates in late Eighteenth Century Scotland", in *EcHR*, second series, vol. XXIV, 1971.

Nisbet, J. W. "Thomas Chalmers and the Economic Order", in *SJPE*, vol. II, June, 1964.

Paul, J. Balfour. "On Beggars' Badges, with Notes on the Licensed Mendicants of Scotland", in *Proceedings of the Society of Antiquaries of Scotland*, 1886-87, vol. IX, new series.

Rose, Michael. "The Allowance System", in *EcHR*, 1966, pp. 607-20.

Thesis:

Cage, R.A. "The Scottish Poor Laws, 1745-1845", unpublished Ph.D. Thesis, Glasgow, 1974.

Lindsay, Jean. "The Operation of the Poor Law in the North-East of Scotland, 1745-1845", unpublished Ph.D. Thesis, Aberdeen, 1962.

MacLaren, A. A. "Religion and Social Class in mid-Nineteenth Century Aberdeen", unpublished Ph.D. Thesis, Aberdeen, 1971.

Roach, William M. "Radical Reform Movements in Scotland from 1815 to 1822, with particular reference to Events in the West of Scotland", unpublished Ph.D. Thesis, Glasgow, 1970.

Smith, C. F. "The Attitude of the Clergy to the Industrial Revolution as reflected in the First and Second Statistical Accounts", unpublished Ph.D. Thesis, Glasgow, 1953.

Nasmyth, Campbell, 97, 105.
New Lanark, 59.
New Town, 64.
Noel, Sir Gerard, 70.
North Leith, 52.

Occasional poor, 10, 14, 34, 113, 143, 149, 154.
Orkney, 116.
Orphans, 10, 17, 19, 29, 39, 48, 56-8, 65, 68, 72, 85, 101, 103, 115, 141, 150, 152.
Out-pensions, 56-7, 62, 65.
Overseers, 41, 48, 77-9, 81, 83-4, 88, 131-2, 155.

Paisley, 12-3, 45, 59-60, 130-2.
Paisley Female Benevolent Society, 73.
Paisley Relief Committee, 60-1.
Parochial, 83-4, 89-90, 94, 98-9, 103-5, 107-8, 111, 117-8, 120-1, 133, 136, 144-6, 152-6.
Parochial Board, 148.
Passes, 41, 144.
Paternalism, iii, 88, 120, 153-4.
Patronage, 133-4.
Pauper(ism), iv, 6, 21, 25, 35, 90-3, 96, 98. 108, 111-5, 117, 119, 123-4, 129, 143-4, 148-9.
Philanthropy, (See private charity).
Private Charity, iii, 27, 29, 42, 60, 67-71, 74-5, 91-2, 120, 128-9, 135, 154-5, 157.
Privy Council, 5, 8.
Provosts, 4-5, 15, 47, 50, 146, 148.
Pollock-Darling, 11-2, 60.
Poor's Fund, 5-6, 24-6, 28-9, 32, 35, 41, 67, 92, 133, 141, 144, 149, 153-4.
Poor Law, i, iii, iv, 1, 15, 21, 41, 76, 79, 86, 112, 115-8, 126, 130, 132-6, 140, 144-5, 147, 150, 152, 155-7.
Poor's List, 34, 113, 117, 143.
Population, i, iii, 45-6, 52, 61-2, 65, 83, 85, 88, 94-5, 98, 113-6, 122-5, 134, 144, 148, 153.
Poverty, i, 87, 90-2, 109, 141, 157.

Rainy, Harry, 105.
Regular Poor, 10-1, 113, 154.
Removal, 4, 79, 80, 115-6, 155.
Report of 1818, iv, 35, 37-8, 112, 114-7, 121-3, 135.
Report of 1839, iv, 35, 38, 117, 121-5, 135, 140.
Report of 1844, iv, 140, 144, 147.
Residence, (See Settlement).
Roxburgh, 116.
Royal Bank, 54.
Rural, iii, 5, 7-8, 15, 19, 37, 111, 153-5.
Ruthwell, 71.

St. Andrew's, 99, 105.
St. Cuthbert's, 50-2, 55, 120.
St. Cuthbert's Charity Workhouse, 58, 63, 119.
St. John's Parish, 49, 90, 94-6, 98-108, 110, 136, 155.
Salton, 31, 33.
Savings Banks, 70-1.
Scottish Parliament, 1, 5, 87,
Secession, 133-4.
Settlement, 4, 16-7, 40-1, 79-81, 97, 103-4, 115-6, 114-5, 149-50, 155.